**PRACTICE
MAKES
PERFECT**

Italian

Sentence
Builder

**PRACTICE
MAKES
PERFECT**

Italian
Sentence Builder

Paola Nanni-Tate

McGraw Hill

New York   Chicago   San Francisco   Lisbon   London   Madrid   Mexico City
Milan   New Delhi   San Juan   Seoul   Singapore   Sydney   Toronto

3 4 5 6 7 8 9 10 11 12 13 14 15 16 17 18 19 20 21 22   WDQ/WDQ   0

ISBN 978-0-07-160035-4
MHID   0-07-160035-3
Library of Congress Control Number: 2008939103

Interior design by Village Typographers, Inc.

McGraw-Hill books are available at special quantity discounts to use as premiums and sales promotions, or for use in corporate training programs. To contact a representative, please e-mail us at bulksales@mcgraw-hill.com.

Contents

Introduction

Writing skills can be difficult to acquire and use effectively in any language. This is particularly true when writing in a foreign language. This book will guide you through the many different structures in the Italian language and show you how to avoid the common pitfalls of writing in a foreign language.

In order to learn to write well, you need considerable practice. This book provides many exercises in which you will put to use the rules that are explained in each chapter. At the end of the book you will also have plenty of opportunities to be creative and come up with your own original sentences.

In addition, an answer key is provided at the back of the book. It includes the answers for the exercises, as well as sample answers for the more creative exercises, to ensure that you are on the right track.

Good sentence writing can be a difficult, but not impossible, task. It requires breaking the habit of translating word for word from your mother tongue and, instead, acquiring a feeling for the particulars of the new language.

It is my wish that this book be your guide to writing with confidence in Italian. Remember that learning a foreign language takes time. Don't be too hard on yourself, and be patient.

In bocca al lupo! (*Good luck!*)

**PRACTICE
MAKES
PERFECT**

Italian
Sentence Builder

Declarative sentences and word order

Phrases and sentences are different in nature and serve different purposes. A phrase is made up of more than one word but does not have a **subject + predicate** structure.

one or more words → phrase subject + predicate → sentence

Phrases are used frequently in colloquial Italian and daily conversations.

A presto.	*See you soon.*
Buon giorno.	*Good morning.*

Below are examples of proverbs or short sayings commonly used in the Italian language. They are phrases because they do not have a subject-verb structure.

Meglio tardi che mai.	*Better later than never.*
A buon intenditor poche parole.	*A few words to the good listener.*

A sentence is an organized idea or thought. It is a grammatical unit consisting of different elements such as nouns, verbal structures, adverbs, modifiers, and object pronouns. Each element contributes to a sentence's structure. A sentence expresses a statement, a question, a command, a wish, or an exclamation. In writing, it generally begins with a capital letter and ends with the appropriate punctuation. In speaking, it is expressed with various stresses, pitches, and pauses. Following is an example of a simple sentence:

subject + predicate

Maria parla l'italiano.	*Maria speaks Italian.*

This sentence consists of a subject (**Maria**) and a predicate (**parla l'italiano**, including the verb **parla**). The subject, the "who" or "what" the sentence is about, is often the first element in a sentence. The predicate expresses the action of the subject.

Declarative sentences

Depending on the action they perform, sentences are classified into categories. First we will examine the declarative sentence. Declarative sentences are simple sentences with one verb in the indicative tense. They state a fact, an idea, or an argument. Declarative sentences make a statement and communicate information; they do not ask questions, express exclamations, or give commands. These sentences use the following elements:

subject + verb + complement

Il volo 237 parte domani.   *Flight 237 will leave tomorrow.*

Take a look at the following sentences:

Il volo 237 **parte** alle dieci di mattina.   *Flight 237 **leaves** at ten in the morning.*
Il volo 237 **è partito** in ritardo ieri.   *Flight 237 **left** late yesterday.*
Oggi, il volo 237 **partirà** alle diciassette.   *Today, flight 237 **will leave** at five in the evening.*

The verbs in these declarative sentences are in the indicative mode of the infinitive **partire**: present **parte**, past **è partito**, and future **partirà**.

ESERCIZIO
1·1

Is it a phrase or a sentence? Write P for phrase or S for sentence.

1. Maria ed io. _P_

2. La porta è chiusa. _S_

3. Noi leggiamo il giornale. _S_

4. Buona notte. _P_

5. Di niente. _P_

6. Questo è certo. _S_

7. Voi viaggiate. _S_

8. Loro aspettano. _S_

ESERCIZIO
1·2

Translate the following sentences into Italian.

1. My brother is very young.

   Il mio fratello è molto giovane

2. He is only eighteen.

   Lui è solo dieci-otto   Ha solo diciotto anni

3. His name is Marco.

   Il suo nome è Marco   Si chiama Marco

4. I spoke to him yesterday.

   Ho parlato con lui ieri

5. He is always on time.

Lui è sempre puntuale po

6. He will call you soon.

Lui Ti chiamerà presto

7. She reads many books.

Lei legge molti libri.

8. We like Rome.

Noi Ci piace Roma

9. We want to visit new places.

Noi vogliamo visitare porti nuovi

10. You (pl.) are interested in learning a new language.

Voi siete interesanti ad imparare una lingua nuova.

Word order in declarative sentences

In every language, words must be arranged in the proper and logical order to express ideas clearly and to avoid misunderstandings. In Italian, as in English, the natural word order of simple sentences is:

subject + verb + direct object

Giovanna compra il libro.   _Giovanna is buying the book._

This is the most frequent word order in Italian, but unlike English, Italian allows for more flexibility. Another pattern commonly used in Italian is:

verb + subject

Venne un temporale.   _A storm came._

Some declarative sentences are expressed with an indirect object noun instead of a direct object noun.

subject + verb + indirect object

Maria parlerà a Luigi.   _Maria will speak to Luigi._

Declarative sentences with direct and indirect object nouns

In English and Italian alike, some declarative sentences include both direct and indirect object nouns.

subject + verb + direct object + indirect object

Renata ha comprato un libro a suo padre.   _Renata has bought a book for her father._

The word order is the same in the Italian and English sentences, but in English you can also say:

Renata has bought her father a book.

This word order shows that English has more flexibility than Italian when direct and indirect object nouns are used in a sentence.

Declarative sentences with direct and indirect object pronouns

Although the word order in declarative sentences with object *nouns* is similar in both English and Italian, there is a significant difference between the word order in the two languages when using direct and indirect object *pronouns*. In Italian sentences, all object pronouns are placed before the verb.

subject + indirect object + direct object + verb

Renata gliel(o)' ha comprato.   *Renata bought it for him.*

ESERCIZIO
1·3

Write complete sentences using the following words and phrases.

1. vive / Maria / in questo palazzo

   Maria vive in questo palazzo

2. è / Lucia / la moglie / di Pietro?

   Lucia, è la moglie di Pietro?

3. di Marco / sulla spiaggia / la casa / è

   La casa di Marco è sulla spiaggia

4. rientrano / Lucia e suo marito / dalle vacanze

   Lucia e suo marito rientrano dalle vacanze

5. la notizia / abbiamo letto / del tuo matrimonio / sul giornale

   Abbiamo letto la notizia del tuo matrimonio sul giornale.

6. i film / ti piacciono / di fantascienza

   Ti piacciono i film di fantascienza

7. la televisione / guardate / alla sera?

   Guardate la televisione alla sera?

8. glielo / portate / quando?

   Quando glielo portate?

9. non andiamo / telefoniamo / spesso / ma

   Non andiamo, ma telefoniamo spesso.

10. del caffè / la tazza / sul tavolino / è

    La tazza del caffè è sul tavolino.

Declarative sentences with prepositional phrases

Sentences may include a variety of prepositional phrases such as **di sera** (*in the evening*), **all'ombra** (*in the shade*), **per i tuoi amici** (*for your friends*). Generally these phrases will occupy the same position in both Italian and English sentences. Compare the following:

Noi andiamo **ai corsi serali**.	*We attend **night classes**.*
Tu ti siedi **all'ombra**.	*You sit **in the shade**.*
Durante la cena, guardiamo la televisione.	***During dinner**, we watch television.*

Be aware of phrases such as **i corsi serali** (*the night classes*). Note how **corsi** (*classes*) comes before **serali** (*night*). Compound phrases such as this follow reversed word order in Italian than in English. When you encounter these phrases, remember that the Italian phrase will position the main idea (the fact that it is a class) first, followed by the detail (it is an evening class). These examples follow the same pattern:

il cucchiaino da caffè	*the coffee spoon*
la casa di campagna	*the country home*
gli occhiali da sole	*the sunglasses*
il tempo estivo	*the summertime*

Declarative sentences with adverbial phrases or adverbs

It is normal to use the same word order in Italian and in English when dealing with an adverbial phrase.

adverbial phrase + subject + verb

Tutte le sere noi usciamo.	*Every night we go out.*

Or:

subject + verb + adverbial phrase

Noi usciamo tutte le sere.	*We go out every night.*

Though an adverbial phrase such as **tutte le sere** (*every night*) can appear either before or after the subject-verb cluster in the Italian and English sentences, there are a few phrases, such as **a mano** (*by hand*), that only appear after the subject-verb cluster in both languages.

Noi cuciamo **a mano**.	*We sew **by hand**.*

Simple adverbs in Italian can have a variety of positions in a sentence. Longer adverbs (more than two syllables), can be found at the beginning or at the end of a sentence. When placed at the beginning of a sentence an adverb is usually emphatic.

Adesso, ne ho abbastanza.	***Now**, I have had enough.*
Ne ho abbastanza **adesso**.	*I have had enough **now**.*

The most common position for an adverb, especially for short adverbs (no more than two syllables), is right after the verb in an Italian sentence. This is different from its most common position in English sentences, which is before the verb.

subject + verb + adverb + complement

Lei fa sempre il suo lavoro.	*She always does her work.*

Compare the positions of the adverbs in the following Italian and equivalent English sentences.

Tu parli **spesso** con tua sorella.
Lei studia **anche** l'inglese.

You **often** speak with your sister.
She **also** studies English.

As you can see, the adverb is placed before the verb in English but after it in Italian.

ESERCIZIO
1·4

Translate the following sentences into Italian.

1. Today we study Italian.

    Oggi noi studiamo l'Italiano

2. We speak Italian well.

    Noi parliamo bene l'italiano

3. We already finished reading.

    Abbiamo già finito di leggere.

4. I rarely study.

    Studio raremente

5. I will bring it to him tonight.

    Glielo porterò questa sera.

6. We always talk about Italy.

    Parliamo sempre dell'Italia

7. She gives me coffee, too.

    Mi da anche il caffè.

8. I bring a book to my sister.

    Porto un libro ad mia sorella.

9. We often get together to have a party.

    Noi spesso

10. You (sing.) live in the country, but love the city.

    Vivi in la campagna, ma amire la città

Negative declarative sentences

To make an affirmative sentence negative in Italian, place the word **non** directly in front of the conjugated verb.

Leggiamo molto.
→ **Non** leggiamo molto.

We read a lot.
We do **not** read a lot.

| Lei balla bene. | She dances well. |
| → Lei **non** balla bene. | She does **not** dance well. |

| Il treno è arrivato. | The train arrived. |
| → Il treno **non** è arrivato. | The train did **not** arrive. |

There is no equivalent for the auxiliary words *do*, *does*, and *did* in Italian. Do not try to include them in a negative Italian sentence.

Other common negative words or phrases (adverbs) that are used to create negative declarative sentences are: **niente** (*nothing*), **mai** (*never*), **mai più** (*never again*), **neppure** (*neither*), **nè** (*neither, nor*), and **da nessun parte** (*nowhere*). Unlike English, two or three negative words can be used in a single Italian sentence.

Non so **niente**.	I do **not** know **anything**. (I know **nothing**.)
Noi **non** viaggiamo **mai** in inverno.	We **never** travel in winter.
Non vuole **più** fumare.	He does **not** want to smoke **anymore**.
Lei **non** mi invita **mai** alla festa.	She **never** invites me to the party.
Io **non** voglio **mai più** fare del male.	I do **not** want to do **anything** bad **again**.
Io **non** fumerò **mai più**.	I will **never** smoke **again**.
Elisa **non** viaggia **mai**.	Elisa **never** travels.

In Italian the negative pronouns **nessuno** (*no one*) and **alcuno** (*someone*) also appear with other negative words.

Domani **non** viene **nessuno**.	Tomorrow **no one** will come.
Non c'è **alcun** problema.	There is **no** problem.
Lucia **non** chiede **niente**.	Lucia does **not** ask for **anything**.

In Italian, to be emphatic you may use redundant elements, or double negatives, in a sentence, especially in informal conversations.

| Maria **non** verrà **mai** e poi **mai**. | Maria will **never ever** come. |

ESERCIZIO
1·5

Affirmative or negative? Write A for affirmative and N for negative.

1. Le palme sono alte e belle. _A_

2. La luna non brilla oggi. _N_

3. Vedo molte stelle nel cielo. _A_

4. Di notte, gli uccelli dormono sugli alberi. _A_

5. Mai e poi mai starò a dormire in questo albergo. _N_

6. Nessuno dice niente. _N_

7. Non mi piace la gente che fuma. _N_

8. Lui ha paura di viaggiare in aereo. _A_

9. Abbiamo molto da fare. _A_

10. Non c'è niente che io voglia comprare. _N_

Translate the sentences from Esercizio 1-5 into English.

1. The palms are tall and beautiful
2. The moon is not bright today
3. I see many stars in the sky.
4. At night, the birds sleep under the tree
5. _____
6. Nobody says anything
7. I do not like people who smoke
8. He is afraid of travelling in the air
9. We have alot to do
10. _____

Double negatives. Add another negative word to the following sentences.

1. _____ e poi mai avremo un anno così prospero.

2. Non vediamo _____ molta gente dalla finestra.

3. Giulia non invita _____ a casa sua.

4. Non ho mangiato nè il pesce _____ la carne.

5. Non lo dice a _____ .

6. Io non faccio più _____ questa sera.

7. Non dire a _____ quello che ti ho raccontato.

8. Non fa _____ dalla mattina alla sera.

9. _____ mi piace nè mangiare nè bere nei ristoranti che non conosco.

10. _____ vengono all'ora giusta. _____ capiscono niente.

Write the following sentences in Italian using only one negative word.

1. I never buy wine at this store.

   _____

2. The clerk is never very helpful.

   _____

3. Maria does not play with anybody.

   _____

4. I do not like to watch baseball or football on television.

   _____

5. Neither you nor I feel very well.

   _____

6. You never play tennis.

   _____

7. The children in this neighborhood never play outside.

   _____

8. The students in Italian schools do not have sports or theater.

   _____

9. This city is not near the sea or the mountains.

   _____

10. My job is never boring.

   _____

Interrogative sentences

Interrogative sentences ask a question. In English an interrogative sentence can be formed by adding the helping verbs *do*, *does*, or *did* before the subject in a declarative sentence:

Marco likes good food.	→	**Does** *Marco like good food?*
They just got married.	→	**Did** *they just get married?*

In Italian a **declarative** sentence can become an **interrogative** sentence by placing the subject after the verb:

verb + subject

Legge Giovanni?   *Does Giovanni read?*

The auxiliary words *do*, *does*, or *did* used in English to form a question are not used in Italian. Italian has no such helping verbs.

Forming interrogative sentences

There are three types of interrogative sentences, those that:

◆ Elicit a yes-no response

Luisa è a casa?	*Is Luisa at home?*
Sì?/No?	*Yes?/No?*

These yes-no questions in Italian are formed by placing a question mark at the end of an affirmative sentence in written language. In spoken Italian a different voice intonation is given to signify that a question is being asked. This type of interrogative sentence can also be formed by putting the subject at the end of a sentence.

Luisa è a casa? (asking tone in the voice)	*Is Luisa at home?*
È a casa **Luisa**? (subject at the end of the question)	*Is Luisa at home?*

◆ Ask for information

Di che nazionalità è Luisa?	*What nationality is Luisa?*

◆ Seek agreement or confirmation

Luisa dorme, non è vero?	*Luisa is sleeping, isn't she?*

In English as well as in Italian you can change a statement into a question by adding a short phrase at the end of the statement. This short phrase is called a **tag question**, or tag, because it is tagged onto the end of a sentence. These questions are intended to elicit consent, agreement, confirmation, or verification. In Italian the words **no** (*no*), **vero** (*true/right*), **non è vero** (*isn't it right/isn't it correct*), and **giusto** (*right*) can be added or tagged onto a statement to change it into a question.

Luisa è una brava ragazza, **no**?
Sei molto stanco, **vero**?
Oggi è venerdì, **non è vero**?
Hai capito la lezione, **giusto**?

*Luisa is a nice girl, **isn't she**?*
*You are very tired, **aren't you**?*
*Today is Friday, **isn't it**?*
*You understood the lesson, **right**?*

When using the verbs **essere** (*to be*) and **avere** (*to have*), the question usually begins with the verb.

Sei ancora a casa?
Hai un vestito nuovo?
Sei stato a casa o sei andato a giocare a tennis?
Hai visitato tutti i tuoi parenti in Italia?

***Are you** still at home?*
***Do you have** a new dress?*
***Did you stay** at home or did you go to play tennis?*
***Have you visited/Did you visit** all your relatives in Italy?*

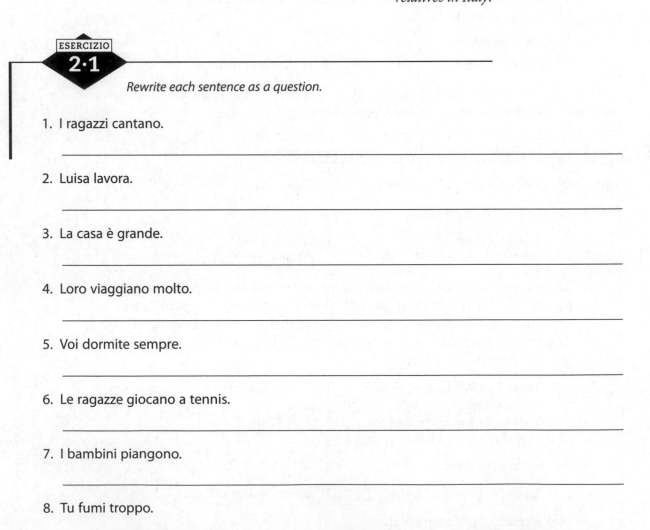

ESERCIZIO
2·1

Rewrite each sentence as a question.

1. I ragazzi cantano.

   _____

2. Luisa lavora.

   _____

3. La casa è grande.

   _____

4. Loro viaggiano molto.

   _____

5. Voi dormite sempre.

   _____

6. Le ragazze giocano a tennis.

   _____

7. I bambini piangono.

   _____

8. Tu fumi troppo.

   _____

9. Maria è andata a casa.

_____

10. La tua amica è ammalata.

_____

Translate the following questions into Italian.

1. Do you (sing.) play basketball?

_____

2. Do you (sing.) smoke a lot?

_____

3. Does Luigi live here?

_____

4. Do you (sing.) speak English?

_____

5. Do the ladies play bridge on Wednesday?

_____

6. Does she travel by train?

_____

7. Are you (sing.) happy in this house?

_____

8. Is your (sing.) father the gentleman whom I met the other night?

_____

9. Do you (sing.) have a lot of stress in your life?

_____

10. Have you (sing.) traveled to many parts of the world?

_____

Rewrite the following questions changing them to Italian tag questions, using the suggestions in parentheses.

1. Tu studi molto (*right*)?

   _____

2. Suo marito è un campione di tennis (*isn't it true*)?

   _____

3. Loro sono in vacanza (*no*)?

   _____

4. Il concerto è sabato (*isn't it*)?

   _____

5. Preferisci il gelato al dolce (*true*)?

   _____

6. Loro vanno in chiesa la domenica (*don't they*)?

   _____

7. È molto scoraggiante perdere sempre (*right*)?

   _____

8. Se uno non paga le tasse, potrebbe andare in prigione (*no*)?

   _____

9. I parchi americani sono molto belli e spaziosi (*aren't they*)?

   _____

10. Bisogna guidare per molte ore per attraversare gli Stati Uniti (*right*)?

    _____

Interrogative words

Interrogative sentences eliciting information use the following words: **chi** (*who*), **che cosa** (*what*), **quando** (*when*), **dove** (*where*), **come** (*how*), **quanto** (*how much*), **quale** (*which*), and **perchè** (*why*). In general, Italian and English interrogative words are used much in the same way. The main interrogative words in Italian are used as follows.

   Chi (*who*) is used in questions to inquire where or to inquire what one or more persons may be doing. It is a singular pronoun and requires a singular verb, even when it refers to a plural subject.

Maria abita in Italia.	*Maria lives in Italy.*
→ **Chi** abita in Italia?	***Who** lives in Italy?*
I miei genitori vivono a Parigi.	*My parents live in Paris.*
→ **Chi** vive a Parigi?	***Who** lives in Paris?*
Il dottore non è ancora arrivato.	*The doctor has not arrived yet.*
→ **Chi** non è ancora arrivato?	***Who** has not arrived yet?*
Luisa e suo marito non conoscono tua madre.	*Luisa and her husband do not know your mother.*
→ **Chi** non conosce tua madre?	***Who** does not know your mother?*

Chi is also frequently preceded by simple prepositions depending on the case of the noun that is being replaced.

a chi	*to whom*
con chi	*with whom*
da chi	*where*
di chi	*whose*
per chi	*for whom*

In the following examples you can observe the use of a **preposition** + *chi*. The subject of the sentence is replaced by the pronoun **chi**.

A chi (*to whom*) is used to ask to whom something is being given, said, or brought.

A chi ha dato il libro?	***To whom** did she give the book?*
Lei ha dato il libro alla sua amica.	*She gave the book to her friend.*

Di chi (*whose*) is used to show possession.

La nonna **di chi** viene in America?	***Whose** grandmother will come to America?*
La nonna di Paola viene in America.	*Paola's grandmother will come to America.*

Da chi (*where*) is used to ask at whose house one is or is going to be.

Da chi sei?	***Where** are you? (**Whose house?**)*
Sono a casa di Luisa.	*I am at Luisa's house.*
Sono da Luisa.	*I am at Luisa's.*
Da chi vai domani?	***Whose house** are you going to tomorrow?*
Vado a casa di mia zia.	*I am going to my aunt's house.*
Vado da mia zia.	*I am going to my aunt's.*

Con chi (*with whom*) is used to ask with whom something is done.

Con chi vai in Italia?	***With whom** will you go to Italy?*
Vado in Italia con la mia famiglia.	*I will go to Italy with my family.*

Per chi (*for whom*) is used to inquire for whom something is done.

Per chi sono questi regali?	***For whom** are these presents?*
Questi regali sono per mio nipote.	*These presents are for my nephew.*

Rewrite the following sentences as questions and change the underlined words or phrases to the appropriate form of **chi** *or* **preposition** + **chi**.

1. Luisa ha un libro per i tuoi figli.

   _____

2. La casa è di mia zia.

   _____

3. Porto il pane alla mia amica.

   _____

4. Vado al cinema con le mie amiche.

   _____

5. Vogliono visitare la nonna.

   _____

6. Quando vado in Florida sto da mio figlio.

   _____

7. Penso spesso a mia mamma.

   _____

8. Domani viene la mia amica.

   _____

The interrogative words **che** and **che cosa** (*what*) are used to replace nouns referring to objects or a group of objects in a sentence. Even if the noun replaced by **che** or **che cosa** is plural, **che** and **che cosa** do not change.

Che cosa vuoi?	**What** *do you want?*
Io vorrei un gelato.	*I would like an ice cream.*
Che cosa compri?	**What** *do you buy?*
Compro molte riviste.	*I buy many magazines.*
Che vuoi mangiare?	**What** *do you want to eat?*
Vorrei mangiare una pizza.	*I would like to eat pizza.*

Come (*how*) is generally used to inquire into someone's name or their health.

Come si chiama quella signora?	**What** *is that lady's name?*
	(literally, **How** *is that lady called?*)
Quella signora si chiama Adriana.	*That lady's name is Adriana.*
Come sta tua zia?	**How** *is your aunt?*
Mia zia sta poco bene.	*My aunt is not feeling well.*

Dove (*where*) is used to inquire about a location.

Dove va lui?	*Where is he going?*
Lui va al mercato.	*He goes to the market.*

The prepositions **da** and **di** are sometimes placed in front of **dove**. *Da dove* + *verb* inquires into the origin or the motion of the subject. **Di** + **essere** (*to be*) inquires about the origin of the subject.

Da dove + verb

Da dove vieni?	*Where are you coming from?*

Di dove + essere

Di dove sei?	*Where do you come from?*
Di dov'è Angela?	*Where is Angela from?*
Angela è italiana.	*Angela is Italian.*
Di dove è Luisa?	*Where is Luisa from?*
Luisa è di Napoli.	*Luisa is from/was born in Naples.*

Here are some additional wayås that **dove** is used in questions:

- **Dove** + location + subject → location (*Where?*)

Dove dorme tuo marito?	*Where is your husband sleeping?*

- **Dove** + verb of motion + subject → motion to a place (*Where to?*)

Dove vanno gli studenti?	*Where are the students going?*

- **Da dove** + verb of motion + subject → motion from a place (*Where from?*)

Da dove arriva il treno?	*Where is the train coming from?*

Quando (*when*) is used to ask when something is going to happen.

Quando arriva l'autobus?	*When will the bus come?*
L'autobus arriva fra dieci minuti.	*The bus will come in ten minutes.*

Quale (*which*) is used to make a distinction between two or more people, things, or animals. The endings change according to the number of the noun that **quale** modifies.

Quale professore è molto bravo?	*Which professor is very good?*
Il nuovo professore è molto bravo.	*The new professor is very good.*
Quali amici vedi oggi?	*Which friends will you see today?*
Oggi vedo i miei amici italiani.	*Today, I will see my Italian friends.*

Perchè (*why*) is used to ask about reasons or motives of actions.

Perchè va dal dottore Luisa?	*Why is Luisa going to the doctor?*
Luisa va dal dottore perchè non si sente bene.	*Luisa is going to the doctor because she is not feeling well.*

Quanto/a/i/e (*how much, how many*) is used to inquire about the quantity of the nouns it modifies. The endings change according to the gender and number of the noun that **quanto** modifies in a sentence.

Quanto caffè bevi durante il giorno?	*How much* coffee do you drink during the day?
Quanta pioggia è venuta?	*How much* rain fell?
Quanti fiori hai comprato?	*How many* flowers did you buy?
Quante piante hai comprato?	*How many* plants did you buy?

When used as a pronoun, **quanto** does not change gender or number.

Quanto leggi?	*How much* do you read?
Quanto camminate?	*How much* do you walk?

Note also that the final vowel of **cosa**, **come**, **dove**, **quando**, and **quanto** may be dropped when these words precede the verb form **è** to make: **cos'è/cosa è**, **com'è/come è**, **dov'è/dove è**, **quand'è/quando è**, **quant'è/quanto è**.

Quand'è il concerto?	*When is* the concert?
Quant'è un cappuccino?	*How much is* a cappuccino?

ESERCIZIO
2·5

Compose four questions for each of the following items, using **quando**, **quale**, **perchè**, *and a tag question. Use either* **bevi** *(you drink) or* **mangi** *(you eat).*

EXAMPLE: il caffè

Quando bevi il caffè?

Quale caffè bevi?

Perchè bevi il caffè?

Bevi il caffè, vero?

1. il gelato

   a. _____

   b. _____

   c. _____

   d. _____

2. il succo di frutta

   a. _____

   b. _____

   c. _____

   d. _____

3. il formaggio

   a. _____

   b. _____

c. _____

d. _____

4. la pasta

   a. _____

   b. _____

   c. _____

   d. _____

5. la cioccolata calda

   a. _____

   b. _____

   c. _____

   d. _____

6. la torta

   a. _____

   b. _____

   c. _____

   d. _____

ESERCIZIO
2·6

Complete the following sentences with the appropriate question words suggested in parentheses.

1. _____ biciclette avete? (*how many*)

2. _____ andate in Italia? (*when*)

3. _____ andate in Italia? (*how*)

4. _____ vestito preferisci? (*which*)

5. _____ vedrai domani? (*who*)

6. _____ giorni starai in vacanza? (*how many*)

7. _____ sono i calzini e le scarpe? (*where*)

8. _____ sta la nonna di Maria? (*how*)

9. _____ è la signora che abita vicino a te? (*where from, born*)

10. _____ arrivano tutte quelle casse divino? (*where from*)

Complete the sentences with the appropriate form, using **chi** *or* **preposition** + **chi.**

1. _____ è quella bella signora?

2. _____ sono queste scarpe?

3. _____ portate il dolce?

4. _____ andate in Italia?

5. _____ dormite quando siete in Italia?

6. _____ fate le lasagne?

7. _____ è quella macchina in garage?

8. _____ comprate la frutta, la pasta e il pane?

9. _____ sono i CD che ho trovato in macchina?

10. _____ dovete parlare oggi pomeriggio?

Complete the following sentences with the appropriate interrogative words.

1. _____ viene la tua amica?

2. _____ desideri comprare al mercato?

3. _____ proviene questa bella statua?

4. _____ delle tue amiche parla l'italiano?

5. _____ vorresti mangiare questa sera?

6. _____ fratelli hai?

7. _____ ragazze giocano a tennis?

8. _____ stivali hai comprato?

9. _____ andate a visitare gli amici che abitano al mare?

10. _____ sono andati gli esami di maturità?

Questions and answers   ·3·

In Chapter 2, you became familiar with the various ways of forming a question in Italian. Nearly every word in a sentence can become a cue for a question to ask and the answer to give.

Forming questions from sentences

Let's look at an English sentence and the questions that can originate from it.

> *Every day after they came home from school, the children played soccer with their friends at the park near their house.*

The following questions are just a few that can be formed from the various elements of this sentence:

> How often did the children play soccer?
> With whom did they play soccer?
> Did the children play soccer every day?
> When did the children play soccer?
> What did the children play every day after school?
> What happened every day after school?

In Italian, too, sentences can be separated into elements, and several questions can be formed. Here is an example:

La madre e il padre di Giovanni vivevano in Italia con la loro figlia maggiore.	*Giovanni's mother and father lived in Italy with their oldest daughter.*

Below are some questions you can form from this sentence. Some questions will:

* Ask about people

Chi viveva in Italia con la figlia maggiore?	*Who lived in Italy with the oldest daughter?*
Con chi vivevano in Italia la madre e il padre di Giovanni?	*With whom did Giovanni's mother and father live in Italy?*

* Inquire about location

Dove vivevano la madre e il padre di Giovanni?	*Where did Giovanni's mother and father live?*

21

Vivevano in Francia con la figlia maggiore la madre e il padre di Giovanni?	*Did Giovanni's mother and father live in France with the oldest daughter?*

◆ Differentiate between persons or things by using **quale** (*which*) or **che cosa** (*what*)

Quale figlia viveva in Italia con la madre e il padre?	*Which daughter lived in Italy with her mother and father?*
Che cosa facevano la madre e il padre di Giovanni?	*What were Giovanni's mother and father doing?*

◆ Use **di chi** (*whose*), to identify possession

La madre e il padre **di chi** viveva in Italia?	*Whose mother and father lived in Italy?*

Some **sì-no** questions seek to clarify information.

La madre e il padre di Giovanni vivevano in Italia?	*Did Giovanni's mother and father live in Italy?*

By understanding how to form questions in this way, you can get all kinds of information. It will also enable you to understand the complexities of a sentence in order to better compose your own. Knowing how to do this effectively will be a great help in compiling proper sentences.

ESERCIZIO
3·1

Write a question for each of the underlined elements in the sentences that follow.

EXAMPLE: I bambini vogliono giocare a scacchi.

Chi vuole giocare a scacchi?

A che cosa vogliono giocare i bambini?

1. La nostra insegnante vuole andare in Italia.

   a. _____

   b. _____

2. Le banche sono chiuse il sabato e la domenica.

   a. _____

   b. _____

3. Il dizionario italiano costa troppo.

   a. _____

4. Io annaffio le piante tutte le sere.

   a. _____

5. Il cane è seduto accanto alla sua padrona.

   a. _____

   b. _____

6. Domani, vado al cinema con le mie amiche.

   a. _____

   b. _____

7. Maria vuole andare a visitare i suoi figli.

   a. _____

8. La macchina è parcheggiata davanti alla casa.

   a. _____

   b. _____

9. Mio marito vuole guardare il torneo di tennis.

   a. _____

   b. _____

10. Mia sorella, mi telefona tutti i giorni.

   a. _____

   b. _____

ESERCIZIO
3·2

Write a complete answer for each of the following questions, using the suggested words or phrases in parentheses.

1. Da dove vieni? (Roma)

_____

2. Quanti ne abbiamo oggi? (12)

_____

3. Che cosa hanno rubato i ladri? (la televisione)

_____

4. Come viaggiano i tuoi amici? (in macchina)

_____

5. Chi viene a visitarti la prossima settimana? (mia sorella)

_____

6. Che cosa fai prima di andare in Italia? (studiare l'italiano)

   _____

7. Di chi sono questi documenti? (miei genitori)

   _____

8. Quando arriva l'aereo? (fra un'ora)

   _____

9. Quanti giornali leggi ogni giorno? (due)

   _____

10. Per chi fai tutti questi costume? (cantanti d'opera)

   _____

Chi and *che cosa*

You have already encountered the interrogative pronouns **chi** (*who*) and **che cosa** (*what*), which are used in questions regarding people and things, respectively. Both pronouns are singular even when they refer to plural nouns.

Chi chiami?	***Who*** *are you calling?*
Che cosa vogliono le tue amiche?	***What*** *do your friends want?*

ESERCIZIO
3·3

Form questions using **chi** *and* **che cosa** *as appropriate, replacing the underlined words.*

EXAMPLE: Luigi parla con mia sorella.

   Chi parla con mia sorella?

1. I bambini devono lavarsi le mani.

   _____

2. Maria deve aspettare Luigi.

   _____

3. Maria deve aspettare i suoi genitori.

   _____

4. Lei ha comprato dei bei fiori.

   _____

5. Ho letto molti libri interessanti.

   _____

6. Mio zio ha perso il <u>portafoglio</u>.

_____

7. Mia zia ha dimenticato <u>dove ha messo la borsa</u>.

_____

8. Penso che <u>questo ristorante sia molto buono</u>.

_____

9. <u>Tutti</u> hanno freddo in classe.

_____

10. Margherita ha lasciato <u>la borsa</u> in classe.

_____

Write an appropriate answer for each of the following questions, using the suggested words or phrases in parentheses.

1. Chi abita con tuo nonno? (la nonna)

_____

2. Che cosa fa tua nonna tutto il giorno? (guardare la televisione)

_____

3. Chi ha telefonato oggi? (il falegname)

_____

4. Che cosa ti ha detto Maria? (non viene a casa mia)

_____

5. Quando va al mercato Carlo? (venerdì mattina)

_____

6. Chi balla molto bene? (Eric)

_____

7. Chi suona molto bene il piano? (il figlio della mia amica)

_____

8. Che cosa vuoi mangiare questa sera? (gli spaghetti)

_____

Use the following words and phrases to form a complete question.

1. viene / con sua sorella / lui / al cinema?

   _____

2. perchè / con i bambini / non giochi?

   _____

3. quanti / ha comprato / metri / la sarta / di stoffa?

   _____

4. quanto / il nuovo CD / costa?

   _____

5. quale / hai comprato / macchina?

   _____

6. avete mangiato / che cosa / questa sera?

   _____

7. al ristorante / a mangiare / siete andati?

   _____

8. da dove / è / questo libro / venuto?

   _____

Write a question using the words in parentheses. Then answer each question.

EXAMPLE: (Che cosa)

Che cosa hai comprato?

Ho comprato una macchina.

1. (Quando)

   a. _____

   b. _____

2. (Perchè)

   a. _____

   b. _____

3. (Da dove)

   a. _____

   b. _____

4. (Chi)

   a. _____

   b. _____

5. (Come)

   a. _____

   b. _____

6. (Da quanto)

   a. _____

   b. _____

7. (Quale)

   a. _____

   b. _____

8. (Quanto)

   a. _____

   b. _____

Imperatives

The imperative is the command form of a verb. It is used to give orders, advice, instructions, encouragements, directions, and suggestions.

Luigi, mangia la carne!	*Luigi, eat the meat!*
Maria, chiudi la finestra!	*Maria, close the window!*
Chiamami, quando hai tempo!	*Call me when you have time!*

In Italian there is a singular and plural form of informal commands (**tu** and **voi**). This is the equivalent of *you* in English. There is also a singular and plural form of formal commands (**Lei** and **Loro**), also equivalent to *you* in English.

(tu) + verb + ! → singular informal command

(Tu) cammina!	*Walk!*

(voi) + verb + ! → plural informal command

(Voi) camminate!	*Walk!*

Lei + verb + ! → singular formal command

Lei cammini!	*Walk!*

Loro + verb + ! → plural formal command

(Loro) camminino!	*Walk!*

-are verbs

First conjugation, or **-are**, verbs drop the infinitive ending **-are** and add the imperative endings, according to person and number. The imperative endings for the first conjugation verbs are: —, **-a**, **-i**, **-iamo**, **-ate**, **-ino**. There is, of course, no first person in the imperative.

	TU	VOI	LEI	LORO
cominciare (to start, begin)	comincia!	cominciate!	cominci!	comincino!
giocare (*to play*)	gioca!	giocate!	giochi!	giochino!
mangiare (*to eat*)	mangia!	mangiate!	mangi!	mangino!
pagare (*to pay*)	paga!	pagate!	paghi!	paghino!
parlare (*to speak*)	parla!	parlate!	parli!	parlino!

(Tu) Parla ai tuoi studenti!	*Speak to your students!*
(Lei) Cominci a parlare!	*Start speaking!*
(Voi) Mangiate tutto!	*Eat everything!*
(Loro) Giochino!	*Play!*

The accent on the third person plural does not fall on the last syllable, but on the first: PAR-li-no and not par-LI-no.

If the infinitive ends in **-ciare** or **-giare**, drop the **-are** and retain the -i. Note, however, that no double **-i** is used with the **-i**, **-iamo**, and **-ino** endings.

If the infinitive ending of the verb is **-care** or **-gare**, drop the **-are**, but add **h** before adding the endings **-i**, **-iamo**, and **-ino**. This is to retain the hard sound of the infinitive.

-ere verbs

Second conjugation, or **-ere**, verbs drop the infinitive ending **-ere** and add the imperative endings according to person and number. The imperative endings for the second conjugation verbs are: **—, -i, -a, -iamo, -ete, -ano**.

	TU	VOI	LEI	LORO
chiedere (*to ask*)	chiedi!	chiedete!	chieda!	chiedano!
scrivere (*to write*)	scrivi!	scrivete!	scriva!	scrivano!
vendere (*to sell*)	vendi!	vendete!	venda!	vendano!

(Tu) Chiedi un favore alla tua vicina!	*Ask your neighbor a favor!*
(Voi) Scrivete bene!	*Write well!*
(Lei) Venda la casa!	*Sell your house!*
(Loro) Chiedano le informazione alla guida!	*Ask the guide for the information!*

-ire verbs

For third conjugation, or **-ire**, verbs, a distinction has to be made between the regular **-ire** verbs and those that add **-isc**. The third conjugation of regular **-ire** verbs drops the infinitive ending **-ire** and adds the following endings according to the person and number: **—, -i, -a, -iamo, -ite, -ano**. The third conjugation verbs that insert **-isc** drop the infinitive ending **-ire** and add the following endings according to person and number: **—, -isci, -isca, -iamo, -ite, -iscano**.

	TU	VOI	LEI	LORO
finire (*to finish*)	finisci!	finite!	finisca!	finiscano!
pulire (*to clean*)	pulisci!	pulite!	pulisca!	puliscano!
sentire (*to hear, listen*)	senti!	sentite!	senta!	sentano!

(Tu) Senti quello che ti dice!	*Listen to what he has to say!*
(Lei) Finisca di parlare al telefono!	*Stop talking on the phone!*
(Voi) Pulite bene le scale!	*Clean the stairway well!*

The first person plural ending in **-iamo** is used more as an exhortation or a suggestion rather than a command.

Andiamo alla stazione!	*Let's go to the station!*
Compriamo una macchina nuova!	*Let's buy a new car!*
Finiamo di lavorare in giardino!	*Let's stop working in the yard!*

Irregular imperative forms

There are several irregular imperative forms. They can be confusing and need to be memorized.

	TU	LEI	NOI	VOI	LORO
andare (*to go*)	va' (vai)	vada	andiamo	andate	vadano
avere (*to have*)	abbi	abbia	abbiamo	abbiate	abbiano
bere (*to drink*)	bevi	beva	beviamo	bevete	bevano
dare (*to give*)	da' (dai)	dia	diamo	date	diano
dire (*to tell, say*)	di'	dica	diciamo	dite	dicano
essere (*to be*)	sii	sia	siamo	siate	siano
fare (*to do, make*)	fa' (fai)	faccia	facciamo	fate	facciano
rimanere (*to stay*)	rimani	rimanga	rimaniamo	rimanete	rimangano
salire (*to go up*)	sali	salga	saliamo	salite	salgano
sapere (*to know*)	sappi	sappia	sappiamo	sapete	sappiano
scegliere (*to choose*)	scegli	scelga	scegliamo	scegliete	scelgano
stare (*to stay*)	sta' (stai)	stia	stiamo	state	stiano
tenere (*to keep*)	tieni	tenga	teniamo	tenete	tengano
uscire (*to go out*)	esci	esca	usciamo	uscite	escano
venire (*to come*)	vieni	venga	veniamo	venite	vengano

ESERCIZIO
4·1

*Rewrite the following infinitives as imperatives in all the appropriate forms (**tu**, **Lei**, **Loro**).*

1. bere _____

2. aspettare _____

3. ordinare _____

4. stare _____

5. votare _____

6. leggere _____

7. mangiare _____

8. sapere _____

9. essere _____

10. mettere _____

Addressing groups

The infinitive of the verb is used to give instructions, warnings, notices, and messages to groups or people in general. These commands can appear on signs or be heard over loudspeakers. When giving a negative command, place **non** in front of the infinitive as shown below.

Non fumare!	*No smoking!*
Non gettare oggetti dal finestrino!	*Do not throw objects from the window!*
Accendere i fari in galleria!	*Turn on the lights in the tunnel!*
Parlare piano!	*Speak softly!*
Osservare il limite di velocitá!	*Mind the speed limit!*

ESERCIZIO
4·2

Translate the following commands into Italian using the imperative form that addresses people or groups.

1. Push! _____

2. Pull! _____

3. Do not touch! _____

4. Keep off the grass! _____

5. Do not speak to the driver! _____

6. Do not take pictures! _____

7. No passing! _____

8. No parking! _____

9. Do not feed the animals! _____

10. Keep the door closed! _____

Lasciare in the imperative form

The verb *lasciare* (*to let*) + **the infinitive** often is used as a command. It is used with **tu, Lei, voi,** and **Loro**.

lasciare + infinitive + !

Lascia stare!	*Let it go!*
Lasciami dormire!	*Let me sleep!*
Lascia passare la signora!	*Let the lady go by!*
Lasci parlare gli altri!	*Let the others speak!*
Lasciate andare la corda!	*Let go of the rope!*
Ci lascino parlare!	*Let us speak!*

The **noi** form with **lasciare** is used in Italian but not in the English equivalent.

Lasciamoli andare a dormire!	*Let's let them go to sleep!*

*Translate the following sentences into English, using **let** or **let's** as appropriate.*

1. Andiamo al cinema!

_____

2. Lascialo viaggiare in Europa!

_____

3. Lasciala parlare!

_____

4. Scriviamo una lettera alla nonna!

_____

5. Lascia che faccia quel che vuole!

_____

6. Lascia che parli io!

_____

7. Andiamo a prendere un caffè!

_____

8. Lasciami mangiare!

_____

9. Ci lascino leggere!

_____

10. Facciamo una foto!

_____

11. Lasci parlare gli altri!

_____

12. Lasciami stare!

_____

Negative imperatives

To form the negative imperative, add **non** before the verb. All the imperative forms, except the **tu** form, use the same conjugations in the negative that are used in the affirmative. For example:

Non pianga!	*Do not cry!*
Non aspettate gli altri!	*Do not wait for the others!*
Non partiamo così in fretta!	*Let's not leave so fast!*

The **tu** form of the negative imperative, however, is formed by inserting **non** just before the infinitive of the verb.

non + infinitive + !

non cantare!	*Do not sing!*
Canta con il coro!	*Sing with the choir!*
→ Non cantare con il coro!	*Do not sing with the choir!*
Scrivi una lunga lettera!	*Write a long letter!*
→ Non scrivere sul muro!	*Do not write on the wall!*
Cammina lentamente!	*Walk slowly!*
→ Non camminare così velocemente!	*Do not walk so fast!*

Imperatives with object and reflexive pronouns

Object pronouns and reflexive pronouns are attached to the end of the **tu**, **noi**, and **voi** forms of the imperative.

Guarda**mi**!	*Look at me!*
Svegliamo**ci**!	*Let's wake up!*
Scrivete**la**!	*Write it!*

However, they are placed before the **Lei** and **Loro** imperative forms.

Mi scriva presto!	*Write to me soon!*
Si accomodino!	*Make yourself comfortable!*

When **Loro** is used with the meaning of *to them*, it is placed after the imperative, is never attached to it, and is not capitalized.

Da' loro la macchina!	*Give (to) them the car!*

When **da'**, **di'**, **fa'**, and **va'** are followed by an object pronoun, the initial consonant of the pronoun is doubled and the accent is dropped.

da**mmi**	*give me*
di**lle**	*tell her*
fa**cci**	*do me*
sta**mmi** vicina	*stay close to me*
va**cci** a prendere una birra	*go get us a beer*

Gli is an exception, however. **Dagli** (*give him*), not da**ggli**, and **digli** (*tell him*), not di**ggli**, are the correct forms.

In the negative forms of the imperative, the positions of the pronouns **Lei** and **Loro** would be before **non**. However, they are omitted and used only for emphasis.

| (Lei) Non mi parli! | Do not speak to me! |
| (Loro) Non si fermino qui! | Do not stop here! |

In the **tu** form, the object pronouns can either be attached to the infinitive or precede it.

Non **mi** aspettare!	Do not wait for me!
or Non aspettar**mi**!	
Non **mi** scrivere!	Do not write me!
or Non scriver**mi**!	

This is also possible with **noi** and **voi**, but the tendency is to place the pronouns at the end of the imperative. **Non scriveteci!** is preferable to **non ci scrivete!**

ESERCIZIO
4·4

Change the following sentences into the negative imperative.

1. Mangiate tutti i cioccolatini!

   _____

2. Compriamo le ciliege!

   _____

3. Fate la doccia!

   _____

4. Saluta il professore!

   _____

5. Facciamo gli esercizi!

   _____

6. Chiama un tassì!

   _____

7. Parla lentamente!

   _____

8. Mettete la giacca!

   _____

9. Comprate una giacca pesante!

   _____

10. Impara a usare il computer!

   _____

Complete the sentences below with the imperative forms of the verbs in parentheses.

1. Per favore, _____ a bassa voce! (Lei-parlare)

2. _____ ai tuoi genitori! (tu-scrivere)

3. Prima di uscire _____ le finestre! (voi-chiudere)

4. Signora, _____ le scarpe! (Lei-provare)

5. _____ perchè avete gli esami! (voi-studiare)

6. _____ la tavola! (tu-preparare)

7. _____ il riso per mezz'ora! (Lei-cuocere)

8. _____ il vino per gli ospiti! (tu-comprare)

9. _____ il dottore. Viene subito! (Loro-aspettare)

10. _____ se tutte le finestre sono chiuse! (tu-controllare)

Complete the following sentences with the imperative forms of the verbs in parentheses.

1. Mamma _____, oggi cucino io! (riposarsi)

2. Non _____ dal letto, sei ancora molto debole! (alzarsi)

3. _____ a cena da noi! (voi-fermarsi)

4. Signora, _____ allo sportello numero 5! (rivolgersi)

5. Mi raccomando _____ prima di uscire! (tu-pettinarsi)

6. Domani _____ prima, se volete andare a pescare! (voi-svegliarsi)

7. _____ bene, fa molto freddo! (voi-coprirsi)

8. _____ da questa parte! (Loro-accomodarsi)

9. Non _____ di dare da mangiare al cane! (voi-dimenticare)

10. Non _____ troppi vestiti! Li comprerà in Italia. (Lei-portare)

Rewrite the following sentences, replacing indirect and direct objects with indirect and direct object pronouns.

EXAMPLE: Da' a lei le matite colorate!

Dalle le matite colorate!

1. Di' a lei che lui l'ama!

   _____

2. Stai vicino a me!

   _____

3. Di' a noi chi viene alla festa!

   _____

4. Da' a me la borsa!

   _____

5. Da' a noi un colpo di telefono!

   _____

6. Fa' a noi un favore!

   _____

7. Fa' a lui un regalo per il suo compleanno!

   _____

8. Non dare a lui un orologio!

   _____

9. Da' a lei la macchina nuova!

   _____

10. Non dare a lei la macchina fotografica!

    _____

Coordinating conjunctions

Conjunctions show how words or phrases are related and allow us to express, in a logical way, a complex thought. If we did not use them, we would end up with a list of disjointed information.

Le pesche **e** le albicocche sono belle **e** buone.	*Peaches **and** apricots are beautiful **and** good.*
La tua casa è bella, **ma** è troppo grande.	*Your house is beautiful, **but** it is too big.*

A clause is made up of a group of words containing a subject and a predicate.

subject + predicate

La vita è bella.	*Life is beautiful.*

Coordinating conjunctions join words, phrases, or clauses of the same type. There are different types of coordinating conjunctions in Italian. They all, though, follow this basic pattern:

word/phrase/clause + conjunction + word/phrase/clause

Io visito le chiese e i musei.	*I visit the churches and the museums.*

Types of conjunctions

Positive coordinating conjunctions join words, phrases, and clauses of equal importance. They include **anche** (*also, too*), **cioè** (*in fact, that is*), **dunque** (*so, therefore*), **e** (*and*), **inoltre** (*besides*), **invece** (*instead*), **ma** (*but*), **perciò** (*so, for this reason*), **però** (*but*), and **pure** (*also*).

Maria compra patate **e** spinaci.	*Maria buys potatoes **and** spinach.*
Il dolce è buono, **ma** io non posso mangiarlo.	*The cake is good, **but** I cannot eat it.*
Ho finito di studiare, **perciò** vado a dormire.	*I finished studying **so** I am going to sleep.*
Io sto a casa **invece** tu vai a ballare.	*I stay at home; you, **instead**, will go dancing.*
Mi piacciono le pesche e **anche** le ciliege.	*I like peaches and cherries **too**.*
Io capisco quello che dici; **cioe'** ti capisco bene.	*I understand what you are saying; **in fact** I understand you well.*

39

Dunque, ditemi quando arriverete.	*So, tell me when you will arrive.*
Ci piace viaggiare, **pero'** non andiamo lontano.	*We like to travel, **but** we do not go very far.*

Negative coordinating conjunctions join words or phrases of equal importance in the negative: **nè… nè** (*neither . . . nor*), **neanche** (*not even*), **nemmeno** (*not even*), and **neppure** (*nor*).

Non ti ho visto e **neppure** ti ho parlato.	*I did not see you, **nor** did I speak to you.*
Non ha bevuto **nè** vino **nè** birra.	*He drank **neither** wine **nor** beer.*
Non vuole andare in montagna e **nemmeno** al mare.	*He does not want to go to the mountains **or even** to the beach.*

Some conjunctions join words or phrases in contrast with each other: **o** (*or*), **altrimenti** (*otherwise*), **oppure** (*or*), and **ovvero** (*or*).

Uscirete questa sera, **oppure** starete a casa?	*Are you going out this evening, **or** will you stay at home?*
Prendete le chiavi di casa, **altrimenti** dovrete aspettare fuori.	*Take the house keys; **otherwise**, you will have to wait outside.*
Andrai all'università **o** andrai a lavorare?	*Are you going to college **or** will you work?*

Others join a phrase or an independent sentence that needs clarification: **cioè** (*that is*), **difatti** (*in fact*), **infatti** (*in fact*), **ossia** (*that is*), **in effetti** (*in reality*), and **vale a dire** (*exactly*).

Me ne andrò tra due giorni, **cioè** giovedì.	*I will leave within two days, **which is** Thursday.*
Non capisco la matematica, **infatti** ho preso un brutto voto nella verifica.	*I do not understand Math; **in fact**, I did not do well on the test.*
Domani sarà un brutto giorno, **ossia** un giorno pieno di riunioni.	*Tomorrow is going to be a bad day; **in fact**, it is full of meetings.*

Some coordinating conjunctions join phrases or independent sentences that indicate a conclusion: **dunque** (*therefore*), **perciò** (*therefore*), **per questo** (*for this reason*), **pertanto** (*for this reason*), and **quindi** (*therefore*).

Ho finito di parlare, **quindi** me ne vado.	*I finished speaking; **therefore**, I will leave.*
Abbiamo mangiato tardi, **perciò** non abbiamo fame.	*We ate late; **for this reason/therefore**, we are not hungry.*
Ho un forte mal di testa, **per questo** non vengo alla festa.	*I have a bad headache; **for this reason**, I am not going to the party*
Oggi ho del tempo libero, **dunque** taglierò l'erba.	*Today I have some free time; **therefore**, I will cut the grass.*

Still others serve to emphasize the coordination between two words, phrases, or sentences: **entrambi** (*both*), **non solo… ma anche** (*not only . . . but also*), **sia… che** (*either . . . or*), **nè… nè** (*neither . . . nor*).

Entrambi Maria ed io andremo in Italia.	***Both** Maria and I will go to Italy.*
Sia mio marito **che** io possiamo portarti a scuola.	***Either** my husband **or** I can take you to school.*
Non solo è alto, **ma anche** robusto.	*He is **not only** tall **but also** stocky.*
Non voleva **nè** nuotare **nè** giocare a tennis.	*He **neither** wanted to swim **nor** play tennis.*

Conjunctions *ma* and *e*

The most commonly used coordinating conjunctions in Italian are **ma** (*but*) and **e** (*and*). Here you will find some practical suggestions for where to place a comma when using them.

- The coordinating conjunction **ma** must be preceded by a comma when it links two opposing sentences or phrases.

Hai preparato la tavola, **ma** ti sei dimenticato i tovaglioli.	*You set the table, **but** you forgot the napkins.*

- **Ma** is not preceded by a comma if it links two elements in the same sentence.

Ho mangiato un panino piccolo **ma** buono.	*I ate a small **but** good sandwich.*

- Finally, **ma** can never be used with **bensì** or **però**. You must use one construction or the other.

È bello **però** caro.	*It is beautiful **but** expensive.*
or È bello **ma** caro. (*never* **ma però**)	

- When listing several items in a sentence, a comma is used before the coordinating conjunction **e**.

In questo bosco vivono cinghiali, cervi, volpi, **e** lepri.	*Wild boars, deer, foxes, **and** hares live in these woods.*

- A comma is used after **e** when an incidental phrase is inserted into the sentence.

In questa foresta è facile vedere il picchio **e**, se si è fortunati, si vede anche la civetta.	*The woodpecker is easily seen in this forest, **and**, if one is lucky, one can see the owl, too.*

- If the word following **e** starts with a vowel, **e** becomes **ed** to make pronouncing it easier.

Tu **ed** io andiamo al mercato.	*You **and** I will go to the market.*

Be careful not to abuse the use of conjunctions. This could fragment your speech and make it less elegant and flowing. The repeated use of **cioè**, **va be'**, **però**, **quindi**, one after the other, is incorrect and not a good representation of spoken Italian.

ESERCIZIO
5·1

Complete each of the following sentences with the appropriate coordinating conjunction.

1. Gli spinaci sono nutrienti _____ contengono ferro.

2. Gli spinaci sono nutrienti, _____ non mi piacciono.

3. L'ho chiamato due volte, _____ non mi ha risposto.

4. L'ho chiamato due _____ tre volte.

5. Vado in vacanza, _____ vi penserò molto.

6. I compiti sono difficili, _____ proveremo a farli.

7. Non sto molto bene, _____ rimango a casa.

8. Il sole di agosto è molto forte, _____ devi mettere il cappello.

9. Gli amici _____ i parenti possono rendere la vita molto difficile.

10. Il vento ha alzato il tetto della casa, _____ dobbiamo ripararlo.

ESERCIZIO
5·2

Combine the following sentences, linking each with the proper conjunction.

1. Ci sono tanti nostri amici. Vorremmo che venissi anche tu.

   _____

2. Ti ammonisco. Fa quel che vuoi.

   _____

3. Segui il tuo istinto. Non venire a piangere da me.

   _____

4. Filippo non è generoso. È molto tirchio.

   _____

5. Franco è un ragazzo molto intelligente. Franco è un genio.

   _____

6. Tu vuoi andare al cinema. Io non voglio di andarci.

   _____

7. I miei genitori non vogliono comprarmi un cane. Non vogliono comprarmi un gatto.

   _____

8. Se tutto va bene mi comprerò la moto. Mi comprerò la macchina l'anno prossimo.

   _____

9. Abbiamo comprato la frutta e la carne. Abbiamo dimenticato il pane.

   _____

10. Lui non sta molto bene. Deve andare dal dottore per un controllo.

    _____

ESERCIZIO
5·3

Circle the correct coordinating conjugation for each of the following sentences.

1. Sono contenta del tuo progresso, però / ma però devi studiare di più.

2. Chiudi la porta o / e la finestra.

3. Ti ho già detto di no, quindi / anzi non insistere.

4. Tua sorella arriva sempre in ritardo perciò / ma deve essere punita.

5. Domani arriveremo a Roma cioè / però partiamo oggi.

6. Giovanni è alto, bello, invece / e famoso.

7. È dimagrita molto però / anche mangia sempre.

8. Non riesco a concentrarmi ma / invece continuo a studiare.

9. La tigre si muove silenziosamente quindi / e velocemente.

10. Scivolò e / invece cadde sul pavimento di marmo.

ESERCIZIO
5·4

Translate the following sentences into Italian using the appropriate coordinating conjunctions.

1. Both Luigi and I will go to the party.

_____

2. Money and power do not bring happiness.

_____

3. She gave us presents, and she invited us to her house.

_____

4. He was tired, and he was not feeling well.

_____

5. I have finished my homework, therefore I can go out to play.

_____

6. I will see you all in two weeks, or for Christmas.

_____

7. The thief moved quickly and quietly.

_____

8. Neither you nor I will be able to go to the wedding.

   _____

9. Today it was very cold, in fact it snowed.

   _____

10. Will you go out with your friends or with your relatives?

    _____

Subordinating conjunctions

Subordinating conjunctions join elements of unequal importance. They join a clause to the main clause; in other words, they subordinate one clause to another. In this chapter, we'll look at the most commonly used subordinating conjunctions grouped according to their use.

main + subordinating + verb + dependent
clause conjunction clause

Andiamo prima che cominci piovere.	*Let's go before it starts raining.*

Common subordinating conjunctions

Conjunctions of cause express a relationship between the dependent and the main clauses.

dal momento che	*because*
dato che	*since, because*
giacchè	*since*
perchè	*because*
poichè	*since, because*
siccome	*since, because*

Sono arrivata in ritardo **perchè** c'era troppo traffico.	*I arrived late **because** there was lots of traffic.*
Dato che ritorno domani, non porto la valigia.	*Since I will return tomorrow, I will not take a suitcase with me.*
Siccome piove, dobbiamo comprare un ombrello.	*Because it is raining, we have to buy an umbrella.*
Dato che l'autobus è pieno, vado a piedi.	*Because the bus is full, I will walk.*

Conjunctions of choice introduce a choice of action between the main and the dependent clauses.

anche se	*even if*
piuttosto che	*rather than*
sebbene	*even*

Giocano al calcio, **sebbene** piova.	*They play soccer, **even** in the rain.*
Ti aspetto **anche se** arrivi tardi.	*I will wait for you **even if** you arrive late.*

Piuttosto che andare in metropolitana, lei va con la bicicletta.

Rather than going on the subway, she's going to ride her bike.

Conjunctions of comparison introduce a dependent clause that expresses a comparison between the main and the dependent clauses.

così… come	*as . . . as*
meglio… che	*better . . . than*
meno… di	*less/fewer than*
più… che	*more . . . than*
piuttosto che	*rather than*
tanto… quanto	*as much . . . as*

Vado a teatro **piuttosto che** il cinema.
*I will go to the theater **rather than** the movies.*

È **meglio** leggere **che** guardare la TV.
*It is **better** to read **than** watch TV.*

Il mare è **tanto** misterioso **quanto** incantevole.
*The sea is **as much** mysterious **as** it is enchanting.*

È **meglio** ridere **che** piangere.
*It is **better** to laugh **than** cry.*

Oggi sulla spiaggia c'è **meno** gente **di** ieri.
*Today at the beach there are **fewer** people **than** yesterday.*

Conjunctions of condition introduce a dependent clause that indicates the necessary conditions for the action expressed in the main clause to happen.

a meno che	*unless*
a patto che	*on condition that*
anche se	*even if*
purchè	*as long as*
qualora	*when*
se	*if*

Se vieni, ci divertiremo.
If you come, we'll have fun.

Qualora tu voglia andare al cinema, fammelo sapere.
When you want to go to the movies, let me know.

Vengo **purchè** tu mi aspetti.
*I will come **as long as** you wait for me.*

Anche se non c'è nessuno, io vado lo stesso.
Even if nobody is there, I'll go anyway.

Conjunctions of contrast express a contrast between the main and the dependent clauses.

al contrario	*on the contrary*
anche se	*though, although*
invece	*while, instead*
ma	*but*
salvo che	*except, unless*

Compra tanti gioielli **anche se** non ha soldi.
*She buys a lot of jewelry, **although** she does not have any money.*

Anche se sarai lontana, ti verrò a trovare.
Though you will be far away, I will come to visit you.

Tutti saranno in classe, **salvo che** nevichi.
*Everybody will be in class **unless** it snows.*

Interrogative conjunctions introduce a subordinating clause that expresses an indirect question or a doubt.

come	*how*
perchè	*why*
quando	*when*
quanto	*how much*
se	*if*

Vorrei sapere **come** si chiama quella ragazza.	*I would like to know what the name of that girl is.* (literally, **how** *that girl is called*)
Non so **quanto** disti il paese.	*I do not know* **how far** *it is to town.*

Conjunctions of location express the relative location discussed between the main and the dependent clauses.

dove	*where*
ovunque	*anywhere*

Ti raggiungerò, **ovunque** tu sia.	*I will reach you,* **wherever** *you are.*

Conjunctions of reason introduce an explanation between the main and the dependent clauses.

come	*as*
comunque	*anyhow*
dato che	*because*
perchè	*because, why*
quantunque	*though, although*
siccome	*since*

Bisogna fare **come** dicono i genitori.	*You must do* **as** *your parents say.*
Comunque vadano le elezioni, io sarò contento.	**However** *the election goes, I will be happy.*
Vorrei sapere **perchè** ti sei fermato.	*I would like to know* **why** *you stopped.*
Se vuoi venire, vieni, **comunque** ti aspetto.	*If you want to come, come;* **anyhow,** *I will wait for you.*

Modal conjunctions introduce a subordinate clause that defines the way in which the action expressed in the main clause is carried out.

come	*as*
come se	*as if*
comunque	*whichever way*
nel modo che	*in the way which*
quasi	*almost*

Fai **come se** fossi a casa tua.	*Our home is your home.* (literally, *Do* **as if** *you were in your home.*)
Comunque tu parli, non ti capisco.	**Whichever way** *you speak, I do not understand you.*

Conjunctions of result or effect establish the result between a main clause and the dependent clause.

affinchè	*so that*
a meno che	*unless*
così	*so*
così che	*so that*
in modo che	*in order that*

Ti dò la chiave, **in modo che** tu possa entrare.	*I will give you the key **so that** you can go in.*
Restavamo nascosti, **affinchè** non ci vedesse.	*We were hiding, **so that** he would not see us.*
Ti telefono **a meno che** non ci vediamo.	*I will call you, **unless** we see each other.*

Conjunctions of time show the relative time between the main and the dependent clauses.

allorchè	*when*
appena	*as soon as*
come	*as soon as*
da quando	*since*
dopo che	*after*
fino a che	*until*
mentre	*while*
ogni volta che	*every time that*
prima che	*before*
quando	*when*
una volta che	*once*

Arrivò a casa, **quando** già dormivamo tutti.	*He arrived home **when** we were all already asleep.*
Prima che si laurei, passerà tanto tempo.	***Before** he gets his degree, a long time will go by.*
Ogni volta che ti guardo, sorrido.	***Every time that** I look at you, I smile.*
Mentre voi studiate, noi ci riposiamo.	***While** you study, we will rest.*
Fino a che non studiate il congiuntivo, non saprete parlare bene l'italiano.	***Until** you study the subjunctive, you will not speak Italian well.*

As you may have noticed from the previous lists, many subordinating conjunctions assume different meanings depending on the context in which they are used. Let's take **come** as an example, first as a conjunction of time:

conjunction (time) + dependent clause + main clause

Come venisti da me andasti a dormire.	*As soon as you came to my house, you went to sleep.*
Come aprì la porta, fu accolto dagli amici esultanti.	***As soon as** he opened the door, he was greeted by his very happy friends.*
Come vennero a casa, andarono a dormire.	***As soon as** they came home, they went to sleep.*

Now let's see **come** used as a subordinating indirect interrogative conjunction:

main + subordinating indirect + dependent
clause   interrogative conjunction   clause

Dimmi come riesci a capirli.	*Tell me how you can understand them.*
Dimmi **come** stai oggi.	*Tell me **how** you are feeling today.*
Vorrei sapere **come** vanno le cose.	*I would like to know **how** things are going.*

Here, **come** is used as a modal subordinating conjunction:

main + modal subordinating + dependent
clause   conjunction   clause

Ho risposto come mi hai suggerito.	*I answered as you suggested.*
Ho fatto **come** mi hai detto.	*I did **as** you asked me to.*

Subordinating conjunctions with indicative and subjunctive moods

Subordinating conjunctions require the verb to be in either the indicative or the subjunctive mood depending on the circumstances. In the majority of cases, subordinating conjunctions of time (**allorché**, **mentre**, **quando**) and cause (**appena**, **dal momento che**, **dato che**, **ogni volta che**, **siccome**) use the verb in the indicative mood.

indicative verb + conjunction (time) + dependent clause

Portami quei documenti quando puoi.	*Bring me the documents when you can.*
Ogni volta che vado a sciare, mi diverto molto.	***Each time that I go*** *skiing, I have a lot of fun.*
Appena tu ritorni dal tuo viaggio, vogliamo vedere le fotografie.	***As soon as you come back*** *from your trip, we want to see the pictures.*
Portami le fotografie **quando vieni**.	*Bring me the pictures **when you come**.*

All of the following subordinating conjunctions require the verb to be in the subjunctive: **a condizione che**, **affinchè**, **benchè**, **nonostante**, **per quanto**, **purchè**, **qualora**, **sebbene**.

conjunction + subjunctive verb + independent clause

Nonostante tu pulisca sempre, la casa è ancora sporca.	*Even if you clean all the time, the house is still dirty.*
Benchè sia intelligente, non si applica.	***Although he is*** *intelligent, he does not apply himself.*
Qualora tu voglia venire, fammelo sapere.	***When you want*** *to come, let me know.*

ESERCIZIO 6·1

Complete the following sentences with the appropriate subordinating conjunctions suggested in parentheses.

1. Sono tutta bagnata _____ pioveva e non avevo l'ombrello. (*because*)

2. Decisi di andare a scuola _____ avessi il raffreddore. (*even if*)

3. Siamo andati via _____ finisse la partita. (*before*)

4. Andremo a casa _____ vi abbiamo accompagnati alla stazione. (*after*)

5. Vengo a casa tua _____ studiamo. (*as long as*)

6. _____ non chiude la porta disturberà tutti. (*if*)

7. Ci ha detto _____ era molto stanco. (*that*)

8. Sono andati via _____ si annoiavano. (*because*)

Complete the following sentences with the appropriate subordinating conjunctions.

1. Vorrei sapere _____ stanno i tuoi amici.

2. _____ abbia molto da studiare, trova il tempo per lo sport.

3. Dimmi _____ non riesci a studiare alla sera.

4. Alcuni studenti sono in ritardo _____ hanno perso l'autobus.

5. Lo spettacolo fu _____ bello _____ tutti uscirono dal teatro molto entusiasti.

6. Non riesco a concentrarmi _____ c'è molta confusione.

7. Mi sono scusata con loro _____ sia molto orgogliosa.

8. _____ la porta sia chiusa, la sentono tutti.

Circle the correct subordinating conjunction for each of the following sentences.

1. Se / E non chiudi la finestra, c'è troppa corrente.

2. Benchè / Perchè tu abbia molto da fare, esci tutte le sere con gli amici.

3. Sono soddisfatta del tuo progresso, ma / ma però devi continuare a migliorare.

4. Ti ho già detto di no ieri, quindi / anzi non me lo chiedere di nuovo.

5. Giovanni viene a casa tardi, perchè / anzi deve finire il suo lavoro.

6. Sebbene / Dopo che vi siete riposati, andremo al mercato.

7. Dimmi se / perchè non riesci a capire l'algebra.

8. Prima che / Dato che tu sei allergica alla polvere, è meglio togliere tutti i tappeti.

Complete the following sentences with the appropriate coordinating or subordinating conjunctions.

1. Io vado, _____ ti aspetto in macchina.

2. _____ tu sappia che sono in macchina ad aspettarti, tu non vieni.

3. Non ho comprato lo zaino _____ mi piacesse _____

   costa troppo, _____ ho deciso di usare quello dell'anno scorso.

4. La squadra ha vinto il torneo di tennis _____ non lo meritasse.

5. Sono molto stanca _____ non mi reggo in piedi, _____
non posso andare a letto _____ ho molte cose da fare.

6. Domani vengono a pranzo i nostri amici, _____ voglio invitare
_____ te e tuo marito.

7. Preferisci usare la bicicletta _____ la motocicletta?

8. _____ tu sia molto sportivo _____ ti piaccia competere,
non vinci mai.

Relative pronouns

A relative pronoun joins a clause, the relative clause, with a larger one, the main clause. As a pronoun it stands in place of a noun or another pronoun previously mentioned in the main clause (its antecedent). Relative pronouns may take the place of the subject, the indirect object, or the object of a preposition. There are fewer relative pronouns in Italian than in English, and determining which one to use depends on its function in the relative clause. Unlike in English, relative pronouns are never omitted in Italian: **che** (*that, who, whom, which*), **chi** (*who, the one who, she who, he who*), **cui** (*that, which, whom*), and **il quale** (*which*).

Che and chi

Che (*that, who, whom, which*) is the pronoun in Italian used for the subject or the direct object of the relative clause.

> **noun + relative pronoun (subject) + relative clause**

La macchina che ha vinto la corsa è mia.	*The car that has won the race is mine.*

> **noun + relative pronoun (direct object) + relative clause**

La macchina che hai visto ieri era mia.	*The car that you saw yesterday was mine.*

Che is the most common relative pronoun. It is invariable for gender and number and is used for persons, animals, and things. **Che** is never used with a preposition. It is placed after the noun that it modifies.

Gli amici **che** sono venuti a pranzo sono molto simpatici.	*The friends **who** came to lunch are very nice.*
La ragazza **che** hai incontrato è Americana.	*The girl **whom** you met is American.*
Il cane **che** abbaia è molto vecchio.	*The dog **that** is barking is very old.*
I biglietti **che** hai comprato sono cari.	*The tickets **that** you bought are expensive.*

Be careful not to confuse the different functions of **che**:

Relative pronoun	L'auto **che** passa è veloce.	*The car **that** is going by is fast.*
Interrogative pronoun	**Che** vuole il tuo amico?	***What** does your friend want?*

Interrogative adjective	**Che** partita hai visto?	**Which** game did you watch?
Exclamative adjective	**Che** meraviglia!	**How** wonderful!
Conjunction	Penso **che** verrò da te.	I think **that** I will come to your house.

Chi (*who, the one who, he who, she who, whoever*) is an invariable, singular pronoun used only for people.

Non so **chi** è al telefono.	I do not know **who** is talking on the phone.
Dobbiamo aiutare **chi** ha fame.	We must help **whoever** is hungry.
Chi viaggia in Italia mangerà molto bene.	**He/She who** travels to Italy will eat very well.

Cui

Cui (*that, which, whom*) is an invariable relative pronoun. It is used as an indirect object when it is preceded by the preposition **a**, or as the object of any other preposition. It is used for persons, animals, and things. If **cui** is used without a preposition, it means **a cui** (*to whom*).

relative clause + indirect object pronoun + main clause

| **Ecco lo studente a cui parlavo in classe.** | Here is the student to whom I was speaking in class. |

Ecco il libro **di cui** ti ho parlato.	Here is the book (**that**) I was speaking of.
Questa è la città **da cui** viene mio padre.	This is the city (**that**) my father comes from.
L'Italia è il paese **in cui** vivo.	Italy is the country where (**in which**) I live.
Il dottore **cui** (**a cui**) parlai è molto conosciuto.	The doctor **to whom** I spoke is very well known.

When **cui** is preceded by the definite article (**il cui, la cui, i cui, le cui**) it has a possessive implication: **definite article +** *cui* = **whose**. **Cui** is invariable, but the definite article must agree in gender and number with the noun that follows it.

possessor + definite article + cui + noun + main clause

| **Ecco la donna il cui figlio canta molto bene.** | Here is the lady whose son sings very well. |

| Ecco la donna **il cui** braccialetto è stato rubato. | Here is the woman **whose** bracelet was stolen. |
| Questa è la mia amica **il cui** figlio ha avuto un incidente con la macchina. | This is my friend **whose** son had a car accident. |

Il quale

Il quale, la quale, i quali, le quali (*who, which, that*) is a variable pronoun used for persons, animals, or things. This form is often replaced in colloquial Italian by **che**. It is used after prepositions for emphasis, for clarification, or to avoid repetition.

L'amica di Maria, **la quale** studia l'inglese, verrà a vivere in America.	Maria's friend, **who** studies English, will come to live in America.
L'uomo, **il quale** legge il giornale, è bene informato.	The man **who** reads the daily newspaper is well informed.
La ragazza **alla quale** porto il regalo, è mia cugina.	The girl **to whom** I bring the gift is my cousin.

Quello *che*, *ciò che*, and *quanto*

Quello che, **ciò che**, and **quanto**, meaning *that which* or *what*, are used when the antecedent is not clear or understood. They are used mostly for things and can be the subject or the direct object of the verb.

main clause + relative pronoun + dependent clause

So quello che è successo ieri a scuola.	*I know **what** happened yesterday in school.*
Non capisco **quello che** dici.	*I do not understand **what** you are saying.*
Fai **ciò che** ti dicono le persone amiche.	*Do **what** friends tell you to do.*
Ecco **quanto** mi ha dato.	*Here is **what** he gave me.*

If **tutto** precedes **ciò che** or **quello che**, it means *all that* or *everything that*.

Se passi gli esami, ti darò **tutto quello che** vuoi.	*If you pass the exams, I will give you **everything** you want.*
Non dice mai **tutto quello che** pensa.	*He never says **all that** he is thinking.*

ESERCIZIO 7·1

*Complete the following sentences with the relative pronouns **che** or **chi**.*

1. Il libro _____ mi hai dato, è appena stato pubblicato.

2. La vita _____ fai è molto faticosa.

3. Ti riporto i biglietti _____ non sono stati venduti.

4. Non conosco la ragazza _____ ti piace.

5. Non so _____ cosa vuoi vedere.

6. Mi dici _____ porti a casa domani?

7. Non parlare con _____ non conosci.

8. Fammi sapere _____ vuoi assumere.

ESERCIZIO 7·2

*Complete the following sentences with the article or appropriate **preposition** + **cui**.*

1. Il film _____ ti ho parlato, è appena uscito.

2. L'Italia è il paese _____ si fanno gli spaghetti.

3. Il ragazzo _____ padre lavora con tuo marito, gioca bene al calcio.

4. Questa è la casa _____ sono cresciuta.

5. L'esame _____ abbiamo studiato, era molto difficile.

6. La classe _____ ci troviamo, è sempre fredda.

7. La signora _____ vuoi fare il regalo, è andata via.

8. Il fatto _____ abbiamo parlato, deve rimanere un segreto.

ESERCIZIO
7·3

Complete the following sentences with the appropriate relative pronouns.

1. L'auto _____ passa è veloce.

2. Rispetto solo _____ stimo.

3. Condivido _____ hai affermato.

4. Potrai conoscere questa sera l'amico _____ ti ho parlato.

5. _____ non sta attento a scuola, non può fare bene i compiti.

6. Il giorno _____ ci siamo incontrati, era d'estate.

7. La fontana _____ ho bevuto, è in montagna.

8. L'uomo _____ mi insegna a sciare, è molto bravo.

Quanto, chiunque, and dove

Quanto in the singular form is used only for things and means *that which, what,* or *all that.* In the plural form, **quanti** and **quante** (*all those that, all those which*) refer to people and things.

Gli dò **quanto** gli spetta.   *I will give him **what** I owe him.*
Quanti verranno saranno i benvenuti.   ***All those that** will come are welcome.*

Chiunque (*anybody, all those who*) is used only for people and always in the singular form.

Chiunque vada alla partita deve avere il   *All those who go to the game must have a*
biglietto.   *ticket.*

Dove is a relative pronoun when it is used to connect two sentences or phrases.

Abita nel palazzo **dove** (**in cui, nel quale**)   *The post office is in the building **where** he*
c'è l'ufficio postale.   *lives.*

Complete the following sentences with the relative pronouns **chi**, **quanto**, **chiunque**,
dove, *or the appropriate form of* **quello che**.

1. Guadagna _____ vuole.

2. Abitano nella città _____ ci sono molti parchi.

3. _____ tace acconsente.

4. Andrà con _____ glielo chieda.

5. _____ va spesso in spiaggia, si abbronzerà.

6. _____ vanno spesso in spiaggia, si abbronzeranno.

7. _____ parli in classe sará punito.

8. Ti dò _____ vuoi.

Complete the following sentences with the appropriate relative pronouns.

1. Il signore _____ è venuto a casa mia, è un collega di lavoro.

2. L'amico _____ mi ha portato in barca, vive molto bene.

3. Non so _____ vuole andare al cinema.

4. Se sapete _____ ha chiamato diteglielo.

5. Il libro _____ ti ho parlato, è molto interessante.

6. La signora _____ porto il regalo, è mia zia.

7. È una persona _____ puoi parlare liberamente.

8. Mangia _____ vuoi.

Complete the following sentences with the appropriate relative pronouns.

1. _____ va piano, va lontano.

2. Il ragazzo _____ studia l'italiano con noi, viene dagli Stati Uniti.

3. Il ragazzo a _____ porto la palla, è molto sportivo.

4. La squadra di calcio _____ ha vinto la coppa del mondo, è italiana.

5. Ecco la signora con _____ parlavo.

6. _____ voglia venire, deve farmelo sapere.

7. Non so _____ volete vedere domani.

8. Questa è la casa _____ sono nato.

Present and past participles

The participle has two forms: present (or simple) and past.

È una donna **affascinante**.	*She is a **fascinating** woman.*
Ho **trovato** il libro.	*I have **found** the book.*

Present participles

In Italian the present participle is formed by adding **-ante** to the stem of **-are** and **-ente** to the stem of **-ere** and **-ire** verbs. The present participle can be used as a noun, as an adjective, and, more infrequently, as a verb.

As a **noun** the present participle is used in the singular or plural form. It is always preceded by the definite or indefinite article: **cantare** (*to sing*) → **il cantante** (*singer*); **amare** (*to love*) → **l'amante** (*lover*); **brillare** (*to shine*) → **il brillante** (*diamond*).

present participle (noun) + verb + direct object

La cantante ha avuto molto successo.	*The singer has had great success.*
Il **cantante** ha lanciato una canzone nuova.	*The **singer** has launched a new song.*
I **cantanti** hanno lanciato la loro canzone nuova.	*The **singers** have launched their new song.*
L'**amante** piangeva, perchè era stata lasciata.	*The **lover** was crying because she had been dumped.*
Il **brillante** luccicava sul suo dito affusolato.	*The **diamond** was shining on her slender finger.*

When the present participle functions as an **adjective**, it is used in the singular and plural forms and in the comparative and the superlative. As an adjective, it expresses a state or an inherent quality of the noun.

subject + verb + direct object + present participle (adjective)

Noi abbiamo visto dei piatti volanti.	*We saw some flying saucers.*
Ho letto un libro **interessante**.	*I have read an **interesting** book.*
Ho letto dei libri **interessanti**.	*I have read some **interesting** books.*
Questo libro è più **interessante** di quello.	*This book is more **interesting** than that one.*
Ho letto un libro **interessantissimo**.	*I have read a **very interesting** book.*

The present participle is used also as a **verb**. However, is not very common in spoken language and tends to be used mainly in political and legal language. The use of a relative clause is usually preferred. A present participle used as a verb has the same value as a relative clause expressing an action contemporary to that indicated by the main verb.

subject + present participle (verb) + dependent clause

I danni derivanti (che derivano) dall'uragano sono enormi.	*The damages caused by (coming from) the hurricane are enormous.*
I soldati hanno trovato una scatola **contenente** (**che conteneva**) una bomba a mano.	*The soldiers found a box **containing** a hand grenade.*
Parleremo con la persona **facente** funzione (**che svolge la funzione**) di presidente.	*We'll speak with the person **functioning** as president.*
È stato firmato il documento **comprovante** (**che comprova**) l'accordo di vendita.	*The document **proving** the sale agreement has been signed.*

ESERCIZIO
8·1

Write the present participles of the following verbs, then translate them into English.

1. assistere _____ _____

2. commuovere _____ _____

3. dirigere _____ _____

4. mancare _____ _____

5. obbedire _____ _____

6. perdere _____ _____

7. riposare _____ _____

8. tollerare _____ _____

9. uscire _____ _____

10. vivere _____ _____

ESERCIZIO
8·2

Complete the following sentences with the appropriate forms of the present participle, using the verbs in parentheses.

1. L'acqua della doccia è _____. (bollire)

2. In questa casa non c'è l'acqua _____. (correre)

3. La ragazza è _____. (sorridere)

4. Mi piacciono i bambini _____. (obbedire)

5. Il mio _____ è una persona molto valida. (assistere)

6. Ha avuto una vita _____. (sconvolgere)

7. Abbiamo visto un film _____. (divertire)

8. L'esercizio è nella pagina _____. (seguire)

ESERCIZIO
8·3

Complete the following sentences with the present participle of the verbs in parentheses functioning as nouns.

1. I _____ di quel paese non sono molto civili. (governare)

2. Luigi è un _____ di una ditta multinazionale. (dipendere)

3. La vita degli _____ è molto dura. (emigrare)

4. I _____ degli autobus oggi sono in sciopero. (condurre)

5. Alcuni _____ hanno visto la rapina. (passare)

6. Questa bevanda è molto _____. (dissetare)

7. I _____ al convegno sono tutti stranieri. (partecipare)

8. Ha acceso gli _____. (abbagliare)

Past participles

Like the present participle, the past participle is used as an adjective, a noun, or a verb. The past participle is formed by changing the endings of regular -**are** verbs (**pagare**, *to pay*) to -**ato** (**pagato**, *paid*). Regular verbs ending in -**ere** (**vendere**, *to sell*) change to -**uto** (**venduto**, *sold*). Regular verbs ending in -**ire** (**capire**, *to understand*) change to -**ito** (**capito**, *understood*). If the verbs have an irregular past participle, it should be used. For example, **scegliere** (*to choose*) would change to the noun or adjective **scelto**.

As an **adjective**, the past participle is used without the auxiliary and agrees in gender and number with the noun it refers to. It is also used in the comparative and the superlative.

subject + past participle (adjective) + verb

I candidati scelti (che sono stati scelti) non piacciono alla popolazione.	*The people do not like the candidates that have been chosen.*
I bambini **viziati** sono molto antipatici.	***Spoiled*** *children are very unpleasant.*
La casa **restaurata** è stata affittata.	*The **renovated** home has been rented.*
La donna **affaticata** voleva riposarsi.	*The **tired** woman wanted to rest.*
L'opera **rappresentata**, ha suscitato molto entusiasmo.	*The opera that was **performed** generated much enthusiasm.*
Il cane è **più amato** del gatto.	*The dog is **loved more** than the cat.*
Il cane è **molto amato**.	*The dog is **loved very much**.*

The past participle used as an adjective is often changed to function as a noun. When it is used as a noun, the past participle does not accompany another noun as it would if it were functioning as an adjective. As a noun it is used as a subject or as an object.

In this example, the past participle **invitati** functions as an adjective modifying a noun:

| I giovani **invitati** sono arrivati tardi alla festa. | *The young people who had been invited arrived late at the party.* |

In the example below, however, the past participle **gli immigrati** functions as a noun:

past participle (noun) + verb + direct object

| **Gli immigrati cercavano un posto per dormire.** | *The immigrants looked for a place to sleep.* |

| Gli **invitati** sono arrivati tardi. | *The **guests** arrived late.* |
| I **laureati** cercavano tutti un lavoro. | *The **graduates** were all looking for a job.* |

The past participle used as a **verb** is added to the auxiliary **avere** or **essere** to form the compound tenses of all the other verbs. It usually expresses actions or events prior to those in the main clause.

subject + avere/essere + past participle

| **Io ho visto.** | *I have seen.* |
| **Io sono visto venuto.** | *I have come.* |

The past participle is also used with the auxiliary **essere** to form the passive constructions.

subject + essere + past participle

| **Noi siamo stati lodati.** | *We have been praised.* |

Past participles standing alone

The past participle is also used by itself as a central element of dependent clauses.

past participle + object + main clause

Raggiunta (Dopo che avevamo raggiunto) **la meta facemmo uno spuntino.**	*Having reached our goal, we had a snack.*
Riposatosi (Dopo che si era riposato) un poco, era pronto per giocare a tennis.	*After resting for a while, he was ready to play tennis.*
Resosi conto che (Siccome si era reso conto) lo avevano riconosciuto, decise di fuggire.	*Realizing that he had been recognized, he decided to run away.*
Rallegrati (Poichè furono rallegrati) dalla notizia, fecero salti di gioia.	*Pleased by the news, they were jumping with joy.*

Often, in front of the past participle one can find the following conjunctions: **appena** (*as soon as*), **benchè** (*even if*), **se pur** (*even if*), **se anche** (*even if*), and **una volta** (*once, when*). These conjunctions help in identifying the type of secondary clause expressed by the participle.

| **Appena arrivata** a casa, telefonò subito alla sua amica. | *As soon as she arrived home, she called her friend.* (appena = *conjunction of time*) |
| **Benchè spaventato**, non respinse il cane. | *Even if he was scared, he did not push the dog away.* |

Generally, the main and the secondary clauses refer to the same subject. If this is not the case, then the subject must be placed directly after the past participle. The past participle must then agree with the subject of the secondary clause.

Persa la partita, i giocatori erano molto silenziosi.	*After losing the game*, the players were very quiet.
Sfumati i soldi, Luigi e Mario decisero di ritornare a casa.	*Once the money was finished*, Luigi and Mario decided to return home.

ESERCIZIO
8·4

Complete the following sentences, changing the verbs in parentheses to past participles used as adjectives.

1. A tutti piacciono molto le patatine _____. (friggere)

2. Con il mare _____ non è consigliabile andare in barca. (muovere)

3. Il corteo avanza _____ dalla banda locale. (precedere)

4. Il tennista _____ dal sole si è ritirato dal torneo. (accaldare)

5. L'acqua _____ del lago viene mandata all'acquedotto. (depurare)

6. Le persone anziane pagano tariffa _____ al cinema. (ridurre)

7. Firenze, una città molto _____ dagli italiani, è molto antica. (amare)

8. Il giocatore di calcio più _____ è brasiliano. (conoscere)

ESERCIZIO
8·5

Complete the following sentences, changing the verbs in parentheses to past participles used as nouns.

1. Li vedo spesso alla _____ dell'autobus. (fermare)

2. Gli studenti non hanno il _____ di parcheggio. (permettere)

3. È necessario il _____ del consolato per entrare negli Stati Uniti. (vedere)

4. All'inaugurazione dello stadio c'erano molti _____. (invitare)

5. Fare un _____ di cipolla, carote, e sedano. (soffriggere)

6. I _____ politici, spesso parlano troppo. (candidare)

7. Questa estate ho avuto molti _____ a casa mia. (ammalare)

8. Lui non sente bene. Ha perso l'_____. (udire)

Rewrite the following sentences using a compound tense in place of the past participle.

EXAMPLE: Terminati gli esami, le bambine andranno in America.

Quando avranno terminato gli esami, le bambine andranno in America.

1. Una volta finito il concerto, ti riporteremo a casa.

_____

2. Spente le luci, la bambina si addormenterà.

_____

3. Finito il corso, gli studenti andranno al mare.

_____

4. Una volta saliti sull'autobus, troveranno senz'altro un posto a sedere.

_____

5. Lavati i piatti, puliranno la cucina.

_____

6. Una volta presa la patente, potranno guidare.

_____

7. Appena arrivati a destinazione, si riposeranno.

_____

8. Finiti i compiti, potranno andare fuori a giocare.

_____

Position of pronouns with the past participle

The pronouns **mi**, **ti**, **gli**, **lo**, **la**, **le**, and the reflexive pronouns **mi**, **ti**, **si**, **ci**, **vi**, **si**, are attached to the end of the participle.

Scritta la lettera e spedita**la**, si sentì molto soddisfatto.	*Once he wrote the letter and he mailed it, he felt satisfied.*
Addormentato**si** sul divano, si svegliò tutto infreddolito.	*After sleeping on the couch, he woke up cold.*

Remember that when the pronouns **lo**, **la**, **li**, **le** precede the compound tenses, the past participle must agree with them.

Li ho vist**i** sulla metropolitana.	*I saw them on the subway.*
Le ho scritt**e** e **le** ho spedit**e**.	*I wrote them, and I mailed them.*

If the pronoun **ne** is used, the past participle must agree with the noun it refers to.

La torta era buonissima, **ne** ho mangiate   *The cake was excellent; I ate two slices of it.*
     due fette.

Rewrite each sentence and replace the underlined phrase with the appropriate pronoun and past participle. Remember where to place the pronoun.

1. Finita la lettera, mi sono sentita sollevata.

   _____

2. Appena riposatosi, viene a visitarvi.

   _____

3. Cercava la palla dappertutto, trovata la palla è uscito a giocare.

   _____

4. Ho letto tutte le tue lettere in questi giorni.

   _____

5. Vedo sempre Marco e Cristina quando ritornano a casa dal lavoro.

   _____

6. La cioccolata calda era squisita, ho bevuto due tazze di cioccolata.

   _____

7. Ho mangiato una banana, ma era acerba.

   _____

8. Ho comprato tante piante.

   _____

Adjectives

9

The word "adjective" comes from Latin *adiectivum*, meaning "word that is added." Adjectives are added to nouns to attribute special qualities to them or to specify some determining aspects of them. Their use makes sentences more interesting, clear, and effective. Adjectives can be attributive or predicative.

Attributive	Ho guidato una macchina **veloce**.	*I drove a **speedy** car.*
Predicative	La macchina è **veloce**.	*The car is **speedy**.*

Attributive adjectives

Attributive adjectives expand or limit the noun they modify. Sometimes these adjectives are placed before the noun and other times they are placed after the noun. We'll look at this later in the unit.

subject + verb + object + attributive adjective

Maria vede gli uccelli affamati.	*Maria sees the hungry birds.*

Ho visto **mio** zio.	*I saw **my** uncle.*
Luisa ha visto un **bel** fiore.	*Luisa saw a **beautiful** flower.*

The adjectives **mio** and **bel** are directly *attributed* to the nouns **zio** and **fiore**. They are placed next to them and have an attributive function.

Predicative adjectives

Predicative adjectives specify a quality or the characteristics of the subject. They refer to the noun indirectly through a verb.

subject + linking verb + predicative adjective

La casa è grande.	*The house is big.*

La bicicletta è **nuova**.	*The bicycle is **new**.*
Francesca sembra **felice**.	*Francesca seems **happy**.*

The adjectives **nuova** and **felice** refer to the noun through the verbs **essere** and **sembrare**.

Adjectives agree in gender and number with the nouns they modify. They can express:

Color	rosso (*red*), verde (*green*), giallo (*yellow*), nero (*black*), violaceo (*purplish*)

Dimension	lungo (*long*), largo (*large*), stretto (*narrow, tight*), grande (*big*), vasto (*wide*), piccolo (*small*), alto (*tall*)
Look	robusto (*stocky*), florido (*florid*), solido (*solid*), liquido (*liquid*), longilineo (*slender*)
Matter	bronzeo (*bronze*), marmoreo (*marble*), ligneo (*wooden*)
Personal feelings	felice (*happy*), triste (*sad*), curioso (*curious*), ansioso (*anxious*), malinconico (*melancolic*), stanco (*tired*), riposato (*rested*), rilassato (*relaxed*), nuovo (*new*)
Physical feelings	caldo (*warm*), freddo (*cold*), dolce (*sweet*), piccante (*spicy*), roccioso (*rocky*), pericoloso (*dangerous*)
Shape	quadrato (*square*), rotondo (*round*), triangolare (*triangular*)
Time	quotidiano (*daily*), diurno (*daytime*), notturno (*nighttime*), serale (*evening time*), invernale (*wintertime*), estivo (*summertime*)

ESERCIZIO
9·1

Write three adjectives to describe each noun, as shown in the example below.

EXAMPLE: finestra <u>quadrata, stretta, nuova</u>

1. libro _____

2. fiore _____

3. casa _____

4. gatto _____

5. montagna _____

6. giornale _____

7. neve _____

8. ragazzo _____

Position of adjectives

Attributive adjectives in Italian sentences can be placed either before or after the nouns they modify. Generally, when the adjective is placed before the noun, it emphasizes the noun it modifies. When it is placed after the noun, the adjective itself is emphasized.

Vidi in lontananza **stanchi** montanari.	*I saw from a distance **tired** mountaineers.*
Vidi in lontananza montanari **stanchi**.	*I saw from a distance mountaineers **who were tired**.*

Often, an adjective placed before the noun it modifies has purely a descriptive meaning. If it is placed after the noun, it is restrictive.

Usa sempre i **vecchi** giocattoli.	*He always uses the **old** toys.*
Usa sempre i giocattoli **vecchi**.	*He always uses the **old** toys.* (the **toys that are old**)

Sometimes the position of an adjective completely changes the meaning.

povero uomo (un uomo di basso livello)	*a man of low station*
uomo **povero** (un uomo senza soldi)	*a man without money*
diverse occasioni (molte occasioni)	*many (several) chances*
occasioni **diverse** (occasioni di vario tipo)	*occasions of different types*

Some adjectives have a fixed position. They are always found after the noun. They are adjectives of:

Color	vestito **blu** (***blue*** *dress*), gonna **rossa** (***red*** *skirt*)
Matter	terreno **sabbioso** (***sandy*** *soil*), roccia **dolomitica** (***dolomite*** *rock*)
Nationality	donna **messicana** (***Mexican*** *lady*), uomo **tedesco** (***German*** *man*)
Shape	cesto **ovale** (***oval*** *basket*), tappeto **quadrato** (***square*** *rug*)

Adjectives that must be altered or changed in form in order to improve a description are placed after the nouns they modify.

donna **magrolina** (*from* **magra**)	***thin*** *woman*
ragazzo **grassotello** (*from* **grasso**)	***plump*** *boy*

ESERCIZIO
9·2

Translate the following sentences into Italian, putting the adjective in the correct position.

1. I saw a poor woman trapped in the snow.

   _____

2. They are American children.

   _____

3. He is an Austrian citizen.

   _____

4. I like square tables.

   _____

5. In Michigan you find sandy soil everywhere.

   _____

6. She wears only black shoes.

   _____

7. I have a red scarf.

   _____

8. She is a sickly person.

   _____

Adjectives used as nouns

The usual function of adjectives is to accompany a noun in order to qualify or determine it better. Sometimes, however, adjectives themselves are used as nouns. In this case, they are preceded by the definite article.

Arrivano **le straniere**. (Arrivano **le donne straniere**.)   *The foreigners are arriving.*

Loro leggono **i gialli**. (Loro leggono **i libri gialli**.)   *They read mystery books.*

Just about any adjective can be used as a noun. Some adjectives are used so often as nouns that it is common to forget their adjectival origins. Here is a list of a few such adjectives:

i belli	*the beautiful*	il possibile	*the possible*
le buone	*good manners*	i poveri	*the poor*
le cattive	*bad manners*	il quotidiano	*the daily (newspaper)*
i deboli	*the weak*	i ricchi	*the rich*
i dolci	*sweets*	i salatini	*salty snacks*
il futuro	*the future*	gli studiosi	*the studious*
le giovani	*the young*	i temerari	*the fearless*
l'impossibile	*the impossible*	i timidi	*the shy*
i mondiali	*the World Cup*	i vecchi	*the old*

ESERCIZIO
9·3

Change the following adjectives into nouns.

1. incerto _____

2. bello _____

3. fiorito _____

4. difficile _____

5. veloce _____

6. nuovo _____

7. caldo _____

8. reale _____

9. velenoso _____

10. profumato _____

11. fresco _____

Complete the following sentences with the adjectives used as nouns suggested in parentheses.

1. I giocatori di calcio del Milan sono chiamati _____. (the red and blacks)

2. La gente spera di poter conoscere _____. (the future)

3. Ogni quattro anni si giocano _____ di calcio. (the World Cup)

4. Agli _____ piace molto l'Italia. (foreigners)

5. _____ e _____ sono molto ammirati. (The rich, the beautiful)

6. La professoressa elogia sempre _____. (the studious)

7. Spesso _____ ottengono più dei _____. (the fearless, weak)

8. _____ hanno sempre paura di tutto. (The shy)

Adverbial adjectives

An adjective that, instead of modifying a noun, modifies a verb is called an adverbial adjective. It is used to better qualify the verb. These include **chiaro** (*in a clear way*), **duro** (*the hard way*), **giusto** (*in the right way*), and **piano** (*in a slow way*). In English these would be considered adverbs, but in Italian they are called adjectives with adverbial value, or adverbial adjectives.

> **subject + verb + adverbial adjective**
> **Lei mangia piano. (in modo lento)** *She eats slowly. (in a slow way)*

The following expressions are part of this group:

Cammina **piano**. (in modo lento)	*She walks **slowly**. (in a slow way)*
Lavorano **sodo**. (in modo sodo)	*They work **hard**. (in a hard way)*
Parla **forte**. (a voce alta)	*He speaks **loudly**. (with a loud voice)*
Parlate **chiaro**! (in modo chiaro)	*Speak **clearly**! (in a clear way)*

Underline the adjectives used as nouns and/or the adverbial adjectives in the following sentences.

1. Gli sportivi devono allenarsi per la gara.

2. Dimmi chiaro e tondo che cosa vuoi.

3. Il piatto toscano più famoso è la classica fiorentina.

4. C'è un proverbio che dice: "Chi va piano, va sano e lontano".

5. Coraggio, il peggio è passato.

6. L'italiano è una lingua difficile da imparare per gli stranieri.

7. Le cinesi lavorano duro nelle fabbriche.

8. Il futuro nessuno lo conosce.

Comparative and superlative forms of adjectives

An adjective used in its regular form is called positive. When an adjective is used to state the idea that someone or something has a relatively equal, greater, or lesser degree of a quality, it is called comparative or superlative.

The comparative is used to express a comparison between two people, animals, or things, in relation to a quality that they both have. The comparative can be of majority, minority, or equality.

The comparative of majority is used when the first term of comparison is greater than the second term of comparison. In this case, the adjective is introduced by **più** (*more*) and the second term is introduced by **di** or **che**.

subject + verb + comparative + adjective + di + second term
of majority   of comparison

Loro sono più affamati di noi.   *They are hungrier than we are.*

Luca è **più calmo di** Marco.   *Luca is **calmer than** Marco.*
Giovanni è **più studioso di** Marco.   *Giovanni is **more studious than** Marco.*
Noi abbiamo **più fame di** te.   *We are **hungrier than** you.*
Lei parla **più velocemente di** suo fratello.   *She speaks **faster than** her brother.*

In the comparative of majority the second term of comparison is introduced by **che** when two nouns, or two noun phrases, are compared by one adjective, noun, or adverb.

subject + verb + comparative + adjective + che + second term
of majority   of comparison

Maria è più affamata che stanca.   *Maria is more hungry than tired.*

Siamo **più** assonnati **che** affamati.   *We are **more** tired **than** hungry.*

The second term of comparison is introduced by **che** in the comparative of majority when:

♦ The second term of comparison is a noun or a pronoun preceded by a compound preposition

   Sei **più** interessato **allo** sport **che allo**   *You are **more** interested **in** sports **than in**
   studio.   *studying.*

♦ Comparing two qualities with the same subject

   È un'occasione **più** unica **che** rara.   *It is an occasion **more** unique **than** rare.*

♦ Comparing two verbs

   È **più** bello dare **che** ricevere.   *It is **better** to give **than** to receive.*

The **comparative of minority** is used when the first term of the comparison is of a lesser degree than the second term. In this case, the adjective is introduced by **meno** (*less*) and the second term is introduced by **di** or **che**, and it follows the same rules as the comparative of majority.

Luca è **meno** alto **di** Marco.	*Luca is **less** tall **than** Marco. (shorter)*
Giulia è **meno** studiosa **che** intelligente.	*Giulia is **less** studious **than** intelligent.*

The **comparative of equality** is used when the quality expressed by the adjective is equally present in the two terms of comparison.

Luca è **tanto** alto **quanto** Marco.	*Luca is **as** tall **as** Marco.*
Lisa è (**così**) simpatica **come** te.	*Lisa is **as** nice **as** you.*

When the quality of the adjective is compared to a group of people or things, the **relative superlative** construction is used. It is formed by placing the definite article in front of **più** or **meno**.

subject + verb + definite + più/meno + adjective + second term
article **of comparison**

Il Sahara è il più grande dei deserti.	*The Sahara Desert is the largest of all deserts.*
Anna è **la più brava** della classe.	*Anna is **the best** of the class.*
Carla è **la meno brava** della classe.	*Carla is **the worst** of the class.*
La Sicilia è **la più vasta** delle isole italiane.	*Sicily is **the biggest** of the Italian islands.*

When the quality of the adjective is expressed in an absolute way, with no comparison, the **absolute superlative** is used. It is formed by adding the suffix **-issimo** to the root of the adjective: bell**o** (*beautiful*) → bell**issimo/a/i/e** (*very beautiful*); urgent**e** (*urgent*) → urgent**issimo/a/i/e** (*very urgent*).

subject + verb + absolute superlative

I pini in California sono altissimi.	*Pine trees in California are very tall.*
La Sicilia è **vastissima**.	*Sicily is **very vast**.*
Il lavoro è **urgentissimo**.	*The job is **very urgent**.*

Other ways to form the absolute superlative of an adjective is by placing the adverb of quality or quantity before the adjective, for example, **molto** (*very*), **davvero** (*really*), or **assai** (*very*).

Mia mamma è **molto stanca**.	*My mother is **very tired**.*

Sometimes the absolute superlative is obtained with prefixes such as:

arci-	arcicontento (*very happy*)
iper-	iperattivo (*hyperactive*), ipercritico (*overly critical*), ipersensibile (*overly sensitive*)
stra-	stragrande (*very big*), stracarico (*very loaded*), strapieno (*very full*)
super-	superaffollato (*overcrowded*), superconveniente (*very convenient*)

Besides the regular formation of comparatives and superlatives, four adjectives have another form that comes directly from Latin:

POSITIVE	COMPARATIVE OF MAJORITY	ABSOLUTE SUPERLATIVE	RELATIVE SUPERLATIVE
buono (*good*)	più buono/migliore	buonissimo/ottimo	il migliore di…
cattivo (*bad*)	più cattivo/peggiore	cattivissimo/pessimo	il peggiore di…
grande (*big*)	più grande/maggiore	grandissimo/massimo	il maggiore di…
piccolo (*small*)	più piccolo/minore	piccolissimo/minimo	il minore di…

The forms **migliore**, **ottimo**, **peggiore**, and **pessimo** are used when:

◆ Referring to something abstract

Devi esercitare un **maggior autocontrollo**. (*not ... un più grande autocontrollo*)	*You must have **more self-control**.*

◆ Using technical and scientific language

Consideriamo **il lato minore** del triangolo.	*Let's take a look at **the shorter side** of the triangle.*

Migliore, **peggiore**, **maggiore**, and **minore** are used with adjectives that describe the ability or the strength of a person.

Ho scelto **il migliore** avvocato della città.	*I chose **the best** lawyer in the city.*
Raffaello è fra **i migliori** artisti italiani.	*Raffaello is one of **the best** Italian artists.*

Six adjectives form the superlative with the suffix **-errimo** rather than the suffix **-issimo**:

acre (*sour*)	acerrimo	integro (*intact*)	integerrimo
aspro (*sour*)	asperrimo	misero (*miserable*)	miserrimo
celebre (*famous*)	celeberrimo	salubre (*healthy*)	saluberrimo

Six other adjectives form the superlative with the suffix **-ente**, which, when put next to **-issimo**, becomes **-entissimo**:

benefico (*beneficial*)	beneficentissimo	malefico (*evil*)	maleficentissimo
benevolo (*benevolent*)	benevolentissimo	malevolo (*malevolent*)	malevolentissimo
maledico (*cursed*)	maledicentissimo	munifico (*munificent*)	munificentissimo

However, the superlatives ending in **-errimo** and **-entissimo** are not commonly used in spoken Italian.

Generally, rather than using the superlative, an adverb precedes the adjective in a sentence.

Le Marche sono una regione **molto salubre**.	*Marche is a **very healthy** region.*
La vitamina C è una vitamina **molto benefica**.	*Vitamin C is a **very beneficial** vitamin.*

ESERCIZIO
9·6

Complete the following sentences in the comparative and the superlative, using the suggestions given in parentheses.

1. Matteo è _____ _____ _____ Mario.
   (*taller*)

2. Matteo è _____ _____. (*very tall*)

3. Lucia legge _____ _____ Giovanna. (*less than*)

4. Lucia legge _____. (*very little*)

5. La minestra è _____ salata _____ carne. (*more ... than*)

6. La minestra è _____ _____ . (*very salty*)

7. La neve è _____ fredda _____ pioggia. (*colder*)

8. La neve è _____ _____ . (*very cold*)

ESERCIZIO
9·7

Using the adjectives and noun phrases provided, form sentences with a comparative, a relative superlative, and an absolute superlative, as shown in the example.

EXAMPLE: La tua amica / simpatica / mia.

La tua amica è più simpatica della mia.

La tua amica è la più simpatica di tutti.

La tua amica è simpaticissima.

1. il gatto / il cane nero / piccolo

    a. _____

    b. _____

    c. _____

2. buono / il dolce / il gelato

    a. _____

    b. _____

    c. _____

3. alto / l'uomo / sua moglie

    a. _____

    b. _____

    c. _____

4. freddo / l'inverno / l'autunno

    a. _____

    b. _____

    c. _____

Complete the following sentences with an appropriate adjective.

1. La tua _____ amica adora la musica classica. (*very young*)

2. La macchina di mio figlio è _____ _____. (*very old*)

3. Questa rivista è _____ _____. (*very interesting*)

4. Sotto le feste di Natale sono _____ _____. (*very busy*)

5. Il ragazzo è _____ _____ _____
intelligente. (*more ambitious than*)

6. Questa città è _____ _____. (*very old*)

7. I miei _____ zii abitano vicino alla torre. (*very old*)

8. I miei vicini sono _____ _____. (*very rich*)

Replace the words in parentheses in each sentence with an adjective.

1. L'acqua (della pioggia) _____.

2. Un bambino (senza vestiti) _____.

3. Un cielo senza nuvole _____.

4. Una minestra (senza sale) _____.

5. Un uomo (privo di lavoro) _____.

6. Un fiore (della primavera) _____.

7. Una regione (senza acqua) _____.

8. Un giovane (senza genitori) _____.

Adverbs

10

The Italian word **avverbio** comes from the Latin *adverbium*, meaning "next to another word." Adverbial expressions can be a single word or a phrase. Adverbs indicate:

Intensity	Maria lavora **davvero molto**.	*Maria works **really hard**.*
Location	Maria lavora **laggiù**.	*Maria works **down there**.*
Manner	Maria lavora **seriamente**.	*Maria works **seriously**.*
Quantity	Maria lavora **troppo**.	*Maria works **too much**.*
Question	Maria, **perchè** lavori?	*Maria, **why** are you working?*
Time	Maria lavora **sempre**.	*Maria works **all the time**.*

Adverbs in Italian are invariable. This means that, unlike adjectives, they never change form to agree with gender or number.

Their function is to modify an adjective, a noun, a verb, or another adverb.

subject + verb + adverb + adjective

Il quadro è piuttosto bello.   *The painting is rather beautiful.*

adverb + noun + adjective + verb

Solo l'attore principale è stato bravo. *Only the main actor was good.*

subject + verb + adverb

Il ragazzo mangia molto.   *The boy eats a lot.*

subject + verb + adverb + adverb

Io ho dormito proprio bene.   *I slept really well.*

Position of the adverb

When an adverb modifies a verb, it is usually placed after the verb it modifies. In compound tenses it can be placed between the auxiliary and the participle.

Camminava **speditamente**.	*He was walking **fast**.*
Ho **molto** gradito il tuo regalo.	*I have appreciated your present **a lot**.*

When an adverb modifies an adjective, a noun, or another adverb, it is usually placed before them in a sentence.

Sei **troppo** debole per fare la partita.	*You are **too** weak to play the game.*
La **quasi** sicurezza del tuo arrivo ci allieta.	*The **near** certainty of your arrival pleases us.*

When the adverb modifies a phrase, it can be placed either before or after the word it modifies.

Il ragazzo **voracemente** divorò la cena.   *The boy **voraciously** devoured dinner.*
Voracemente, il ragazzo divorò la cena.   ***Voraciously**, the boy devoured dinner.*
                             (not very common in English)

Ci (*there*) and **vi** (*there*), as adverbs of location, are placed before the verb.

Ci sono ospiti a casa mia.   ***There** are guests at my house.*
Penso che non **vi** sia nessuno.   *I think that no one is **there**.*

The adverb **non** is placed before what needs to be negated.

L'acqua **non è calda**.   *The water **is not warm**.*

Modal adverbs

Modal adverbs express how an action is carried out by the verb. The majority of adverbs in this category add the suffix **-mente** to the feminine adjective of quality.

feminine adjective + -mente → modal adverb

FEMININE ADJECTIVE		ADVERB	
aperta	*open*	apertamente	*openly*
brillante	*brilliant*	brillantemente	*brilliantly*
certa	*certain*	certamente	*certainly*
forte	*strong*	fortemente	*strongly*
fortunata	*fortunate*	fortunatamente	*fortunately*
generosa	*generous*	generosamente	*generously*
rara	*rare*	raramente	*rarely*
sfortunata	*unfortunate*	sfortunatamente	*unfortunately*

Dobbiamo parlare **apertamente**.   *We have to talk **openly**.*
Fortunatamente, hanno abbastanza da   ***Fortunately**, they have enough to eat.*
    mangiare.

When the adjective ends in **-le**, the final **-e** is omitted before adding the **-mente** ending.

FEMININE ADJECTIVE		ADVERB	
agile	*agile*	agilmente	*agilely*
banale	*banal*	banalmente	*banally*
casuale	*casual*	casualmente	*casually*
generale	*general*	generalmente	*generally*
regolare	*regular*	regolarmente	*regularly*

Other adverbs that end with the suffix **-oni** express positions of the body. They are usually preceded by the preposition **a**.

a bocconi	*facedown*
a carponi	*on all fours*
a cavalcioni	*astride*
a penzoloni	*hanging*

Il bambino gira per la casa **a carponi**.   *The child goes around the house **on all fours**.*
Giovanni siede **a cavalcioni** della poltrona.   *Giovanni sits **astride** the armchair.*

Still other adverbs are the same as the masculine singular of the equivalent adjective.

chiaro	*clearly*
piano	*slowly*
scuro	*dark*
sodo	*hard*
storto	*crookedly*

Lei parla **chiaro**.	*She speaks **clearly**.*
Per favore, fate **piano**!	*Please, go **slowly**!*

Some adverbs do not originate or coincide with adjectives at all.

bene	*well, fine*
così	*so*
insieme	*together*
invano	*in vain*
male	*badly*
volentieri	*willingly*

Il lavoro è fatto **bene**.	*The job is **well** done.*
Vado **volentieri** a scuola.	*I **willingly** go to school.*

Also included among the modal adverbs are the following expressions:

a dirotto	*hard* (as in *raining cats and dogs*)
in fretta e furia	*in a rush*

Adverbs of location

Adverbs of location are used to express where an action takes place or where something is found. Some adverbs in this category are:

davanti	*in front*	quassù	*up here*
dentro	*inside*	sopra	*on (top)*
fuori	*outside*	sotto	*underneath*
intorno	*around*	vicino	*near*
oltre	*further*		

Vieni **quassù**!	*Come **up here**!*
La casa è **vicino** alla strada.	*The house is **near** the street.*

Some useful adverbial expressions of location are:

a destra	*on the right*	di sotto	*under*
a sinistra	*on the left*	nei dintorni	*in the surroundings*
da lontano	*from far away*	per di là	*that way*
di quì	*this way*		

Io non vedo bene **da lontano**.	*I do not see well **from far away**.*
Ci sono molti cipressi in questi **dintorni**.	*There are many cypresses in these **surroundings**.*

Adverbs of time

Adverbs of time express the circumstances, the moment, and the duration of the action expressed by the verb.

adesso	*now*	ora	*now*
ancora	*again*	ormai	*by now*
domani	*tomorrow*	poi	*later, then*
dopo	*after*	recentemente	*recently*
già	*already*	sempre	*always*
giammai	*never*	sovente	*often*
ieri	*yesterday*	subito	*right away*
mai	*never*	tardi	*late*

Stasera andrò a letto **tardi**.
Siamo arrivati **ieri**.

*Tonight I will go to bed **late**.*
*We arrived **yesterday**.*

Here are some helpful adverbial expressions of time:

di quando in quando	*once in a while*	tempo fa	*some time ago*
di solito	*usually*	una volta	*once*
per sempre	*for good*		

Sono stata in Cina **una volta**.
Leggemmo "La Divina Commedia" **tempo fa**.

*I was in China **once**.*
We read The Divine Comedy ***some time ago**.*

Adverbs of quantity

These adverbs express an indefinite quantity:

abbastanza	*enough*	più	*more*
almeno	*at least*	poco	*a little*
appena	*just*	quasi	*almost*
assai	*very much*	tanto	*a lot, much*
circa	*about*	troppo	*too much*
parecchio	*much, several*		

Abbiamo dormito **abbastanza**.
Questo vestito costa **parecchio**.

*We slept **enough**.*
*This dress is **fairly** costly.*

The following adverbial expressions of quantity are quite useful:

a bizzeffa	*a lot*	di più	*more*
all'incirca	*about*	press'a poco	*about*
di meno	*less*	su per giù	*more or less*

Ci sono **su per giù** venti studenti in questa classe.
Luisa ne vuole **di più**.

*There are **more or less** twenty students in this class.*
*Luisa would like **more** of it.*

Adverbs of affirmation, denial, and doubt

This type of adverb reinforces, contradicts, or shows doubt about what is expressed by the verb: It expresses a judgment. Examples of adverbs that reinforce or affirm the verb are:

certamente	*certainly*	proprio	*really*
certo	*sure*	sì	*yes*
esattamente	*exactly*	sicuramente	*surely*

È **certo** che finirò i compiti oggi.

*It is **certain** that I will finish my homework today.*

Vorrei **proprio** andare in centro.

*I would **really** like to go downtown.*

Some adverbs used to express denial regarding the verb are:

neanche	*not even*	no	*no*
nemmeno	*not even*	non	*not*
neppure	*neither*		

Non c'è **neanche** un giornale in questa casa.	*There is **not even** a newspaper in this house.*
Non hai lavato le mani.	*You did **not** wash your hands.*

There is no strict rule about the position of adverbs for affirming or denying, with the one exception of the adverb of denial **non**, which is always placed before the verb.

Some common adverbs used to express doubt are:

circa	*about*	possibilmente	*possibly*
eventualmente	*eventually*	presumibilmente	*presumably*
forse	*maybe*	probabilmente	*probably*
magari	*maybe*		

Probabilmente ci vedremo domani.	*We'll **probably** see each other tomorrow.*
Forse Patrizia starà in Italia per tre settimane.	***Maybe** Patrizia will stay in Italy for three weeks.*

Interrogative adverbs

Interrogative adverbs are used to introduce a direct question.

come	*how, what*	quando	*when*
dove	*where*	quanto	*how much*
perchè	*why*		

Come ti chiami?	***What** is your name?*
Quando andrete in Italia?	***When** will you go to Italy?*

Comparative and superlative of adverbs

Adverbs are compared in the same manner as adjectives; that is, they have three degrees: majority, minority, and equality. Furthermore, adverbs have the relative superlative and absolute superlative constructions, just as adjectives do.

Più, meno, così tanto, come, and **quanto** are used to form the **comparative of majority, minority, and equality**. In all cases they follow this pattern:

verb + più + adverb + second element of comparison

Partirò più tardi di te.	*I will leave later than you.*

Comparative of minority	Partirò **meno tardi** di lui.	*I will not leave **as late as** him.*
Comparative of equality	Partirò **tardi come** lui.	*I will leave **as late as** him.*
Comparative of equality	Partirò **tardi quanto** lui.	*I will leave **as late as** him.*

Molto, assai, and the suffixes **-issimo** and **-issimamente** are used to form the **superlative absolute** construction.

verb + adverb + suffix

Partirò tardissimo.	*I will leave very late.*

You could also say **Partirò molto tardi** or **Partirò assai tardi**.

Il più and **il meno** are placed before the adverb to form the **superlative relative**.

> **verb + il più + adverb + reinforcing element**
>
> **Partirò il più (meno) tardi possibile.**   *I will leave as late as possible.*

Adjectives with irregular forms in the comparative and superlative have the equivalent adverbs with the same irregularities.

ADJECTIVE	ADVERB	COMPARATIVE ADVERB	SUPERLATIVE ADVERB
buono	bene	meglio	benissimo, ottimamente
cattivo	male	peggio	malissimo, pessimamente
grande	grandemente	maggiormente	massimamente
molto	molto	più	moltissimo, assai
piccolo	poco	meno	pochissimo, minimamente

È **tardissimo**, la mamma ci sgriderà sicuramente!	*It is **very late**. Mother will scold us for sure!*
Farò **il meno possibile**.	*I will do **as little as possible**.*
Luigi sta **benissimo**.	*Luigi feels **very well**.*

ESERCIZIO
10·1

Change the following adjectives into adverbs.

1. esatto _____

2. doppio _____

3. ordinato _____

4. freddo _____

5. veloce _____

6. attivo _____

7. allegro _____

8. pacifico _____

ESERCIZIO
10·2

Complete the following sentences with an adjective or adverb as appropriate, using the words in parentheses.

1. I bambini sono _____. (*happy*)

2. I bambini parlano _____. (*happily*)

3. La matematica è una scienza _____ . (*exact*)

4. Lui lavora molto _____ . (*orderly*)

5. È un uomo molto _____ . (*cold*)

6. Parla molto _____ . (*coldly*)

7. La vecchia signora è molto _____ . (*active*)

8. Io lavoro _____ con i miei colleghi. (*actively*)

ESERCIZIO
10·3

Complete each of the following sentences with the appropriate adverb or adverbial phrase.

1. Oggi piove _____ .

2. I bambini sono _____ a giocare.

3. L'autobus si ferma _____ alla scuola.

4. Il cane _____ è tornato a casa.

5. Ti dirò _____ che cosa penso.

6. Tutto è _____ chiaro.

7. Qui nei _____ ci sono molti stranieri.

8. Ci sono _____ cento persone.

ESERCIZIO
10·4

Complete each of the following sentences with a modal adverb.

1. Ti ringrazio _____ .

2. Luisa legge _____ .

3. Maria studia _____ .

4. Lui è entrato in casa _____ .

5. Quel giornalista è _____ invadente.

6. Gli studenti ascoltano _____ .

7. Loro parlano _____ .

8. Lucia e Maria si vedono _____ .

Complete the following sentences with the comparative or superlative of the adverbs in parentheses.

1. Oggi hai fatto il compito _____ _____ di ieri. (diligentemente)

2. Mi è piaciuto _____ lo spettacolo che abbiamo visto. (molto)

3. Stai _____. Che cosa hai fatto? (bene)

4. Vengo da te _____ _____. Adesso devo studiare. (tardi)

5. Vado _____ _____ in gita con i miei amici che con i miei genitori. (volentieri)

6. Ho l'influenza e nonstante io prenda gli antibiotici, oggi sto _____ di ieri. (male)

7. Per le feste sono stata _____. (male)

8. Maria si veste _____ _____. (elegantemente)

Pronouns

11

Pronouns are a variable part of speech that generally replace a noun. They often are used to refer to someone or something that has already been mentioned. Italian pronouns agree in gender and number with the nouns they replace.

> L'uomo → **lui**
> La donna → **lei**
> Il cane → **lui** (**esso**)
> Gli uomini → **loro**

In Italian there is no translation for the pronoun *it*. Instead, everything is considered masculine or feminine. In the "old days" people were referred to by using the pronoun **egli** for masculine nouns and **ella** for feminine nouns, and animals by using **esso/essa**. Today these forms are not used anymore in spoken language. They are found only in written language.

Let us now look at the **personal pronouns**:

SUBJECT PRONOUNS	STRONG PRONOUNS	WEAK PRONOUNS	
io	me	mi	*I, me, me*
tu	te	ti	*you, you, you* (sing.)
lui	lui	lo	*he, him, him (it)*
lei	sè	la	*she, her, her (it)*
noi	noi	ci	*we, us, us*
voi	voi	vi	*you, you, your* (pl.)
loro	loro	li/le	*they, them, them*

Subject pronouns

Keep in mind that the personal pronouns used as the subject of a sentence—**io**, **tu**, **lui**, **lei**, **noi**, **voi**, **loro**—are less frequently used in Italian than in English because the verb in an Italian sentence conveys the agent by its conjugation, making subject pronouns superfluous. Subject pronouns, however, are **not** omitted when:

◆ There is ambiguity about the gender of the subject (especially with the subjunctive)

Lui/Lei gioca.   *He/She is playing.*

- One wants to emphasize something

Voi siete una bella coppia.	*You make a nice couple.*

- There are several subjects

Io lavoro e **lui** si diverte.	*I am working, and **he** is having fun.*

The subject pronouns **io**, **tu**, **noi**, and **voi** are invariable. They are used for the feminine or the masculine. **Io** and **tu** are used for singular forms, while **noi** and **voi** are for plural forms.

Tu sei Alfredo, **tu** sei Luisa.	*You are Alfredo; you are Luisa.*
Noi siamo ragazze, **voi** siete ragazzi.	*We are girls; you are boys.*

Esso/a (*it*) and **essi/e** (*they*) are almost never used.

(Lui) Ha una macchina nuova.	*He has a new car.*
È una Ferrari.	*It is a Ferrari.*
Ha molti libri.	*She has many books.*
Sono tutti nuovi.	*They are all new.*

There is no specific rule to this effect, but usually one does not say **Essa è una Ferrari** or **Essi sono tutti nuovi.**

Remember that Italian has informal versions of you, **tu** (sing.) and **voi** (pl.), as well as formal, **Lei** (sing.) and **Loro** (pl.). They are all used to refer to male or female nouns.

Tu parli bene l'italiano.	*You speak Italian well.*
Carlo, **tu** mi vedi?	*Carlo, do you see me?*
Luisa, **tu** mi vedi?	*Luisa, do you see me?*
Voi parlate bene l'italiano.	*You speak Italian well.*
Carlo e Luigi, **voi** mi vedete?	*Carlo and Luigi, do you see me?*
Luisa e Maria, **voi** mi vedete?	*Luisa and Maria, do you see me?*
Signor Marchi, **Lei** conosce mia sorella?	*Mr. Marchi, do you know my sister?*
Signora Marchi, **Lei** conosce mia sorella?	*Mrs. Marchi, do you know my sister?*
(**Loro**) Si accomodino in quella poltrona!	*(You) Sit in that armchair!*

The formal pronouns **Lei** and **Loro** are always written with a capital letter. **Loro**, however, is only used for emphasis.

Vengano con me!	*Come with me!*
Loro, **vengano** con me!	*You, come with me!*

Personal pronouns as direct objects

Personal pronouns that replace a direct object noun are referred to as **direct object pronouns**.

They are labeled as *weak* (**debole** or **atono**) or *strong* (**forte** or **tonica**). Weak object pronouns are always placed close to the verb, usually in front of it. Strong object pronouns usually follow the verb and they do not need to be placed close to it.

Weak object pronouns get their name because they do not have their own stress. They are pronounced almost in unison with the verb that precedes or follows it.

subject + weak object pronoun + verb

Lui la chiama.	*He calls her.*
Prendo il libro.	*I take the book.*
→ **Lo** prendo.	*I take **it**.*
Vediamo Maria e Giuseppe.	*We see Maria and Giuseppe.*
→ **Li** vediamo.	*We see **them**.*

A strong object pronoun has its own pronounced stress. Strong pronouns create a special strength in a sentence. They clarify and emphasize what the subject wants to convey. They are usually placed after the verb.

subject + verb + strong object pronoun

Luigi chiama lei.	*Luigi calls her.*
Maria chiama **me**.	*Maria calls **me**.*
Maria e Giuseppe chiamano **te**.	*Maria and Giuseppe call **you**.*

The choice between using a strong or weak object pronoun depends on what one wants to relate. If putting emphasis on the pronoun is important, the strong form must be used; otherwise, if no emphasis is needed, the weak pronoun is used.

Per quella partita hanno scelto **me**.	*I was the chosen one for that game.* (The person speaking wants to underline that he/she was preferred to others.)
Mi hanno scelto per quella partita.	*I have been chosen for that game.* (Using the weak pronoun, the person speaking wants only to inform that he/she was chosen.)

ESERCIZIO

11·1

Replace the underlined noun in each sentence with the appropriate object pronoun. Use both the weak and strong forms, as shown in the example.

EXAMPLE: Luisa vede Giovanni tutti i giorni.

Luisa lo vede tutti i giorni.

Luisa vede lui tutti i giorni.

1. Portano mia sorella al cinema.

   a. _____

   b. _____

2. Luisa porta le bambine in piscina tutti i pomeriggi.

   a. _____

   b. _____

3. Contatterò il mio amico appena posso.

   a. _____

   b. _____

4. Portiamo il <u>nostro amico</u> all'aereoporto e poi torniamo a casa.

    a. _____

    b. _____

5. Inviti <u>la professoressa e me</u> a cena a casa tua.

    a. _____

    b. _____

6. Luigi porta <u>i suoi figli</u> in vacanza.

    a. _____

    b. _____

7. Vediamo <u>i tuoi parenti</u> al mare.

    a. _____

    b. _____

8. Rivedo <u>Paolo</u> con molto piacere.

    a. _____

    b. _____

Indefinite pronouns

Indefinite pronouns refer to persons, things, or periods of time that are not well defined. The most commonly used indefinite pronouns are: **uno/una** (*someone*), **qualcuno** (*someone*), **ognuno** (*everyone*), **chiunque** (*whoever*), **chicchessia** (*whoever*), **qualcosa** (*something*), **niente** (*nothing*), **nulla** (*nothing*), **nessuno** (*nobody*).

Uno/una means **una persona** (*someone*). It expresses what people do in general, or is used to point out that the person carrying out an action is unknown. It is used:

◆ To refer to someone unknown

    Ho fermato **uno** e gli ho chiesto dove   *I stopped **someone**, and I asked him where*
    era il museo.   *the museum was.*

◆ To refer to a generic or unknown subject. In this case **uno** is followed by a verb in the third person singular

    In certe situazioni, **uno** non sa cosa dire.   *In some instances, **one** does not know what*
         to say.

◆ Before a relative phrase

    Ho incontrato **uno** che era perso, e l'ho   *I met **someone** who was lost, and I helped him.*
    aiutato.

◆ Before an indirect complement introduced by the prepositions **di**, **del**, **dello**, **della**, **dei**, **degli**, or **delle**

Mi ha telefonato **una della** parrocchia.   *Someone from the parish called me.*
Sei **uno dei** miei migliori amici.   *You are **one of** my best friends.*

ESERCIZIO
11·2

*Rewrite the following sentences using **uno** or **una** as appropriate.*

1. In treno ho parlato con un uomo che non conoscevo.

_____

2. Una persona non sa mai cosa dire ai parenti dei morti.

_____

3. Abbiamo conosciuto una signora che parla bene l'inglese.

_____

4. Un signore ha avuto problemi di cuore mentre era in aereo.

_____

5. Ho parlato con un impiegato dell'anagrafe.

_____

6. Non c'è uno studente in questa classe che capisca la matematica.

_____

7. Ho parlato con una ragazza che non mi piaceva affatto.

_____

8. Maria è una donna che sa il fatto suo.

_____

9. Teresa è fra le mie migliori amiche.

_____

Qualcuno/a (*someone*), **ognuno/a** (*everyone*), **chiunque** (*whoever*), and **chicchessia** (*whoever*) refer to people. They can only be used as pronouns in the singular form.

Quello di cui parli potrebbe farlo **chiunque**.   *Anybody could do what you are talking about.*
Qualcuno vuole venire con me al cinema?   *Someone want to go to the movies with me?*

Complete the following sentences with the pronouns **qualcuno**, **ognuno**, *or* **chiunque** *as appropriate.*

1. Prova a vendere questi libri a _____ che te li comprerà.

2. _____ di voi sa quello che deve fare.

3. _____ voglia venire a Roma con noi, sarà ben accetto.

4. _____ potrà darti precise informazioni quando arrivi alla stazione.

5. _____ pensi di non studiare e imparare, si sbaglia.

6. Voglio portare una rivista italiana a _____ degli studenti.

7. Spero che _____ mi chiami per andare al cinema.

8. Voglio parlare con _____ di voi.

Qualcosa (*something*), **niente** (*nothing*), and **nulla** (*nothing*) are also used only as pronouns and refer only to things.

> Perchè mi sgridi? Non ho fatto **nulla**.   *Why do you scold me? I have not done **a thing**.*
> C'è molta nebbia. Non vedo **niente**.   *It is very foggy. I cannot see **anything**.*

Nessuno (*nobody*) is used only in the singular. In Italian, unlike English, the double negative is frequently used. **Nessuno** is usually preceded by **non**.

> **Non** c'è **nessuno** in casa.   *Nobody is at home.*

Complete the following sentences with **qualcosa**, **niente**, **nulla**, *or* **nessuno** *as appropriate.*

1. Ti assicuro che non ho fatto _____ di male.

2. Sono andata in centro a fare delle compere, ma non ho trovato _____.

3. Vado al mercato perchè ho bisogno di _____ per la cena.

4. _____ vuole comprare i libri usati.

5. Non trovo mai _____ di interessante alla televisione.

6. Il libro di letteratura non piace a _____.

7. Hai comprato _____ di bello in Italia?

8. Non capisco _____.

Reflexive pronouns

When the subject and the object in a sentence are the same person or thing, reflexive pronouns are used. They convey the idea that the action expressed by the verb reflects back to the subject. The reflexive pronoun **si** is used with all the third person (singular and plural) reflexive verbs. Only in the first and second persons are other forms used.

SUBJECT PRONOUNS		REFLEXIVE PRONOUNS	
io	*I*	mi	*myself*
tu	*you*	ti	*yourself*
lui	*he*	si	*himself*
lei	*she*	si	*herself*
Lei	*you*	si	*yourself*
noi	*we*	ci	*ourselves*
voi	*you*	vi	*yourselves*
loro	*they*	si	*themselves*
Loro	*you*	si	*yourselves*

subject pronoun + reflexive pronoun + verb

Io mi lavo.	*I wash myself.*
Tu **ti** svegli presto tutte le mattine.	*You wake (**yourself**) up early every morning.*
Maria **si** veste molto in fretta.	*Maria gets (**herself**) dressed very fast.*
Luigi **si** prepara per andare a lavorare.	*Luigi gets (**himself**) ready to go to work.*

If the infinitive of a verb is preceded by a form of **dovere**, **potere**, or **volere**, the reflexive pronoun is either attached to the infinitive or placed before the conjugated verb.

Mi sveglio presto.	*I wake up early.*
Voglio svegliar**mi** presto.	*I want to wake up early.*
Mi voglio svegliare presto.	*I want to wake up early.*

In compound tenses the auxiliary verb used with reflexive verbs is **essere**. The past participle agrees in gender and number with the subject. The reflexive pronoun is placed before the auxiliary.

subject + reflexive pronoun + **essere** + past participle

Lei si è svegliata.	*She woke up.*

ESERCIZIO 11·5

Complete each of the following sentences with the appropriate form of the reflexive pronoun.

1. Io _____ chiamo Giovanni e tu come _____ chiami?

2. Quelle ragazze _____ alzano tardi.

3. Lei _____ siede vicino al finestrino.

4. Noi _____ addormentiamo sui libri.

5. Voi _____ svegliate presto.

6. Voglio sposar _____ la prossima estate.

7. _____ devo alzare presto per andare al lavoro.

8. Loro _____ vogliono comprare un cappotto pesante.

Infinitives

12

An infinitive is the base form of a verb. In English the infinitive is usually formed by using two words, **to** + **verb**: *to walk*, *to talk*, etc. In Italian, however, the infinitive is composed of only one word, a verb, which ends in -**are**, -**ere**, or -**ire**.

cant**are**	*to sing*
ved**ere**	*to see*
sent**ire**	*to hear*

In an Italian sentence, the infinitive form is used when a verb depends upon another verb other than **essere** (*to be*) or **avere** (*to have*). Usually the preposition **a** or **di** precedes the infinitive. The preposition **da**, however, is found after the verbs **avere** (*to have*), **dare** (*to give*), **fare** (*to make*), **offrire** (*to offer*), and **preparare** (*to prepare*).

verb + a + infinitive

Cominciò a nevicare.	*It started to snow.*
Loro cominciano **a capire** l'italiano.	*They are starting **to understand** Italian.*
Lei pensa di imparare **a volare**.	*She is thinking of learning **to fly**.*
Non pensiamo **di venire** da voi domani.	*We do not think we will **come** to your house tomorrow.*
Non ho niente **da darti**.	*I do not have anything **to give you**.*
Abbiamo molto **da fare**.	*We have a lot **to do**.*

The infinitive is used:

◆ In dependent clauses with verbs that usually require the subjunctive when the subject of the main and the dependent clause is the same

Spero **di vincere** il primo premio.	*I hope **to win** the first prize.*
Pensiamo **di andare** in vacanza in Italia.	*We are thinking **of going** on vacation in Italy.*

◆ In dependent clauses when the verb is in the present tense in the main clause and indicates that the action is going on at the same time or a later time with respect to the verb in the dependent clause

Same time	Spera di **vederlo**.	*She hopes **to see him**.*
Later time	Spera **di vincere** la partita.	*She hopes **she will win** the game.*

- ◆ When the imperative is preceded by the negative **non**.

Non parlare!	***Do not talk!***
Non attraversare i binari!	***Do not cross*** *the tracks!*

- ◆ As a noun preceded by the article **il**. It is always masculine.

Il bere fa male alla salute.	***Drinking*** *damages health.*
Il viaggiare è interessante ma faticoso.	***Traveling*** *is interesting, but tiring.*

- ◆ With certain modal verbs

dovere	*must, to have to*
piacere	*to like*
potere	*to be able, can, to be allowed*
volere	*to want*

subject + modal verb + infinitive + complement

Maria deve stare a scuola.	*Maria has to stay in school.*
Devo aspettarlo fuori della scuola.	***I have to wait for him*** *outside the school.*
Non possiamo parlare al telefono.	***We cannot speak*** *on the telephone.*
Luisa **voleva fare** la modella.	*Luisa **wanted to be** a model.*
Ci **è piaciuto viaggiare** in prima classe.	*We **liked traveling** in first class.*

Tenses of the infinitive

The infinitive has two tenses: **simple** (or present) and **compound** (or past). The simple infinitive corresponds to the English *to* + **verb**.

present infinitive + object + main clause

Ascoltare la musica è rilassante.	*To listen to music is relaxing.*
Sciare è molto divertente.	***Skiing*** *is lots of fun.*
Giocare a tennis è un buon esercizio.	***Playing*** *tennis is good exercise.*
Imparare una lingua straniera fa bene alla mente.	***Learning*** *a foreign language is good for the mind.*

The **past infinitive** expresses an action or a condition valid in the past. It is formed by using the infinitive of the auxiliary **avere** or **essere** followed by the past participle of the verb. **Avere** or **essere** generally drop the final -e.

adverb + past infinitive + main clause

Dopo averlo ascoltato ero stanco.	*After having listened to him I was tired.*
Dopo **esser tornato** dalle vacanze avevo molto da fare.	*After **I returned** from vacation I had a lot to do.*

Rewrite the following sentences using **prima di** *and* **dopo**.

EXAMPLE: Prima telefono poi esco.

Prima di uscire, telefono.

Dopo aver telefonato, esco.

1. Prima chiediamo il prezzo, poi compriamo.

   a. _____

   b. _____

2. Prima chiamo un taxi, poi telefono a Marco.

   a. _____

   b. _____

3. Prima passo di qui, poi vado in chiesa.

   a. _____

   b. _____

4. Prima mi lavo le mani, poi mangio.

   a. _____

   b. _____

5. Prima pensa, poi agisce.

   a. _____

   b. _____

6. Prima mi vesto, poi vado a lavorare.

   a. _____

   b. _____

7. Prima scrive la lettera, poi va alla posta.

   a. _____

   b. _____

8. Prima studiamo, poi giochiamo.

   a. _____

   b. _____

Using the verbs in parentheses, complete each of the following sentences with the present infinitive.

1. Sono contenta di _____ i tuoi fratelli. (*to see*)

2. Questo libro comincia ad _____ noioso. (*to be*)

3. Ma quando imparerete a _____ a bridge? (*to play*)

4. Giovanni ha smesso di _____ . (*to smoke*)

5. Abbiamo l'abitudine di _____ il caffè alle quattro del pomeriggio. (*to drink*)

6. Pensiamo di _____ al mare questa estate. (*to go*)

7. Io comincio a _____ le valige. (*to pack*)

8. Siamo spiacenti di non _____ vi. (*to see*)

ESERCIZIO

12·3

Circle the correct form of the infinitive in each of the following sentences.

1. È stato terribile vedere / avere visto tutta quella povera gente.

2. Dopo pensarci / averci pensato bene, abbiamo deciso di non comprare una macchina nuova.

3. Per arrivare / essere arrivati in tempo alla stazione, dovreste uscire ora.

4. È stato necessario chiamare / aver chiamato il dottore.

5. Dopo aver finito / finire la scuola sono andati al mare.

6. Abbiamo fatto un'ora di coda per aver comprato / comprare i biglietti per il concerto.

7. Prima di passare / essere passati di qui, ci siamo fermata al bar.

8. Per passare / aver passato gli esami, è necessario studiare molto.

ESERCIZIO

12·4

Complete the following sentences with the present or past infinitive of the verbs in parentheses.

1. Dopo _____ della morte del suo amico, si è chiuso in camera sua. (apprendere)

2. Per _____ medico, occorre studiare molti anni. (diventare)

3. Dopo _____ la sua lettera, gli ho telefonato. (leggere)

4. Prima di _____ al mercato, vai in banca. (andare)

5. Dopo _____ il discorso, è andato a comprare il giornale. (finire)

6. Dopo _____ molte volte, mi ha finalmente risposto. (telefonare)

7. Prima di _____ la televisione, finisco i lavori di casa. (guardare)

8. Per _____ un architetto, deve capire la matematica. (diventare)

ESERCIZIO 12·5

Rewrite the following sentences with the modal auxiliary **potere**, *as shown in the example.*

EXAMPLE: Non capisce niente.

Non può capire niente.

1. Sua madre non beve vino.

_____

2. La ragazza non legge mai.

_____

3. Dopo pranzo andiamo a riposare.

_____

4. Lei non apre la porta a nessuno.

_____

5. Noi parliamo con i nostri amici.

_____

6. Lei ha comprato i biglietti per l'aereo.

_____

7. Voi siete andati dal dottore.

_____

8. Io mi faccio la barba tutte le mattine.

_____

Infinitive constructions with *aiutare, imparare, leggere, sentire,* and *vedere*

The verbs **aiutare**, **imparare**, **leggere**, **sentire**, and **vedere** are conjugated in the present or the past tenses and are followed by an infinitive.

Maria mi aiuta a **scrivere** una lettera.	*Maria helps me **write** a letter.*
Hai sentito **cantare** il tenore?	*Did you hear the tenor **sing**?*
Abbiamo visto qualcuno **camminare** in giardino.	*We saw someone **walk** in the garden.*
Ho imparato ad **andare** in bicicletta.	*I learned **to ride** a bike.*

ESERCIZIO
12·6

Complete the following sentences using the verbs in parentheses.

1. Io imparo a _____ la lingua cinese. (*to speak*)

2. Aiuto le persone anziane a _____ . (*to walk*)

3. Sento _____ il campanello. (*to ring*)

4. Devo _____ un albero di Natale. (*to buy*)

5. Lei mi aiuta a _____ la casa. (*to clean*)

6. La bambina vede _____ il suo papà. (*to arrive*)

7. Potete _____ un bel film domani. (*to see*)

8. Avete potuto _____ la segreteria. (*to listen*)

Words with special meaning

13

In every language there are some words added to sentences for emphasis or to make a particular phrase more interesting. Some of these phrases make quite a statement when used in a sentencc. For example:

> I do not want her to come   →   I **certainly** do not want her to come
> with us.   with us!

Italian also has many such expressions. They are used in spoken language and also in writing to make the content more interesting and exciting.

Words used for emphasis

The following words in Italian are used in such a way that makes it impossible to be translated into English and do justice to them.

Dunque is generally used to encourage the conclusion of a statement. It may also be used when one does not know what to say or wants to take some time to express a thought.

Dunque, venite o restate?	*Are you coming or staying?*
Dimmi **dunque**!	*Tell me then!*

Allora is often used to prompt someone to say or do something fast.

Allora, che cosa ha detto?	*What did he say?*
Allora, vieni o no?	*Are you coming or not?*

Quindi is used to express a conclusion to what one is doing or saying.

Piove, **quindi** non usciamo.	*It is raining, so we will not go out.*
Quindi se vuoi, andiamo al mercato.	*If you want, we will go to the market.*

The interrogative **come** (*how, what*) is often combined with other words to form a variety of questions.

Come ti chiami?	*What is your name?*
Come vanno le cose?	*How are things going?*
Come dici?	*What are you saying?*

The adverb **infatti** means *indeed* or *in fact* and is used for emphasis or to make a point in a sentence.

Non so dove andare, **infatti** ho perso la strada.	*I do not know where to go; in fact, I am lost.*
Lei è una professoressa di matematica, **infatti** una bravissima professoressa.	*She is a math professor—in fact, a very good one.*

ESERCIZIO
13·1

*Complete the following sentences using **dunque**, **quindi**, **allora**, **come**, or **infatti** as appropriate.*

1. _____ venite o no?

2. La vita è dura, _____ cerchiamo di viverla il meglio possibile.

3. _____ che cosa avete fatto durante l'estate?

4. _____ mai non avete chiamato vostro padre?

5. Non voglio vedere quel film, _____ l'ho visto già due volte.

6. _____ a che ora ci incontriamo?

7. Sono due ore che aspetto, _____ me ne vado.

8. Io non mi ricordo di lei, _____ non l'ho mai vista!

Mica is a word used mostly in colloquial speech and in informal situations. By itself, it does not reinforce a negative sentence, but rather modifies it. **Mica** is an adverb, and as such, it modifies other adverbs, adjectives, and verbs. It never modifies a noun. It is used with **non** to reinforce the negative. It is difficult to translate, but can mean *in the least* or *at all*. The examples below will help clarify its use:

Il biglietto non era **mica** caro.	*The ticket was not expensive **at all**.*
Io non voglio **mica** correre il rischio di essere in ritardo.	*I do not want to run the risk of being late.*
Il film non mi piace **mica** tanto.	*I do not like the movie so much.*
La mia vita non va **mica** male!	*My life is not bad!*

Mica can be used in negative questions to mean *by any chance*:

Hai **mica** visto le mie chiavi?	*Have you, **by any chance**, seen my keys?*
Non hai **mica** comprato il pane?!	*Have you **by any chance** bought the bread?!*

Mica can often be replaced by **affatto** (*at all, completely*). Both **mica** and **affatto** express strong negative feelings.

Questo vestito **non** mi piace **mica**.	*I do not like this dress **in the least**.*
Questo vestito **non** mi piace **affatto**.	*I do not like this dress **at all**.*

*Complete the following sentences using **mica** or **affatto** as appropriate.*

1. Non penso _____ a te tutto il giorno!

2. Non lo penso _____ .

3. Non mi piacciono _____ i molluschi.

4. Alla bambina non piace _____ il vestito.

5. Non vuoi _____ che porti tutto quel peso!

6. Non ha finito _____ tutti i suoi compiti.

7. Non ci vede _____ .

8. Maria non è _____ molto simpatica.

Già is mostly used as an adverb of time, but it is also used in place of *yes*, to confirm what the speaker has said. In this form it expresses disappointment, irony, and distance.

—Pensi che la colpa sia di Marco? —**Già**.	*"Do you think it is Marco's fault?" "**Yes**."*
—Aspetti da molto tempo? —**Già**.	*"Have you been waiting for a long time?"* *"**Yes**." (answered with an upset tone)*

Su and **giù** are used to point out conditions of emotional well-being, conveying meanings of *good* and *bad*, respectively.

Mi sento **su**. (= Sono allegro./Sto bene.)	*I am happy./I am feeling well.*
Mi sento **giù**. (= Sono triste/depresso./ Sto male.)	*I am sad/depressed./I am not feeling well.*
Tiriamoci **su**. (= Cerchiamo di non essere tristi.)	*Let's try to be happy.*
Non buttarti **giù**. (= Non ti deprimere.)	*Do not get depressed.*
Su con la vita! (= Abbandona la tristezza!)	*Up with life!*

Avanti and **indietro** are used to allude not only to a material location but also to a figurative one, or to encourage someone to do something about his/her status.

Professore, sono rimasto **indietro** con i compiti.	*Professor, I am **behind** on the homework.*
La classe è molto **avanti** rispetto a me.	*The class is far **ahead** in comparison to me.*

Avanti and **indietro** may be used to push someone to move forward or to back up.

Avanti, corriamo!	***Go on**, let's run!*
Indietro, per favore! Non spingete!	***Back up**, please! Do not push!*

Su and **avanti** are also used to press someone to do something.

Su, ragazzi, ridatemi la palla!	***Come on**, boys, give the ball back to me!*
Avanti, non facciamo gli sciocchi!	***Come on**, let's not be silly!*

Complete the following sentences with **su**, **giù**, **avanti**, *or* **indietro** *as appropriate.*

1. _____, cerca di essere ottimista!

2. Oggi non sto bene, mi sento _____.

3. Dobbiamo cercare di stare _____.

4. _____ ragazzi, studiate di più.

5. _____! Non fate troppo chiasso!

6. State tutti _____, per favore!

7. Io sono _____ rispetto alle altre mie compagne di scuola.

8. _____ bambini, finite di mangiare!

Pat phrases

Italian uses many short phrases that are pat responses to someone else's remarks. These phrases can be helpful in conversations with native Italian speakers. The following list shows some of the most commonly used of these pat phrases:

Acqua in bocca!	*Be quiet!*	Fantastico!	*Fantastic!*
Certamente!	*Certainly!*	Forza!	*Courage!*
Che bellezza!	*How wonderful!*	Impossibile.	*Impossible.*
Che peccato!	*What a pity!*	In bocca al lupo!	*Good luck!*
Che sfortuna!	*What a misfortune!*	Magari!	*Maybe!/If only it were true!*
Chiedo scusa!	*Excuse me!*	Mamma mia!	*Mamma mia!*
Coraggio!	*Courage!*	Naturalmente!	*Naturally!*
Davvero?	*Really?*	Non c'è di che.	*Do not mention it.*
Dipende.	*It depends.*	Non ho idea.	*I have no idea.*
Eccellente!	*Excellent!*	Santo cielo!	*For Heaven's sake!*
Ecco!/Ecco fatto!	*That's it!*	Sfortunatamente no.	*Unfortunately no.*
Eccomi!	*Here I am!*	Tu sei matto!	*You are crazy!*
È incredibile!	*Unbelievable!*	Veramente?	*Really?*

A number of these expressions can make an appropriate response to a given statement. For example:

—Ha vinto la medaglia d'oro alle Olimpiadi! —**Fantastico!/Eccellente!/ Davvero?**

"He won the gold medal at the Olympics." "Fantastic!/Excellent!/Really?"

—La donna ha fatto un brutto incidente stradale. —**Santo cielo!/Che sfortuna!/ Veramente?**

"The lady had a bad car accident." "For Heaven's sake!/What a misfortune!/ Really?"

Respond to each of the following sentences with an appropriate pat response.

1. Vuoi andare con noi in Italia? _____

2. Devo fare gli esami prima di finire la scuola. _____

3. Voglio fare il paracadutista. _____

4. Sono entrata in camera, ma non sapevo che stavate dormendo. _____

5. Non dirle quello che ti ho detto. _____

6. Ci siamo riviste dopo quasi trenta anni. _____

7. Le bambine stanno imparando a sciare. _____

8. Vi ringraziamo di tutto. _____

Write a sentence or question that is appropriate for the response given.

EXAMPLE: *Vai in Italia questa estate?*

Sfortunatamente no.

1. _____

Veramente?

2. _____

Non ho idea.

3. _____

Coraggio!

4. _____

Che sfortuna!

5. _____

Eccomi!

6. _____

Eccellente!

7. _____

Magari!

8. _____

Mamma mia!

Idioms and special phrases

·14·

In Italian and English alike, the use of idioms in everyday conversation is very common. A non-native speaker will find these idioms pretty strange and hard to translate because their specific meaning does not correspond to their literal one. It would be hard to translate the English idiom *It is raining cats and dogs* into another language, for example.

ordinary words + unexpected usage → idiom

Using idiomatic expressions

Idiomatic expressions make the language more fun, and you are much closer to being fluent when you can use them successfully. Special phrases like these are made up of a combination of words that are used to express ideas in a way that common translations cannot relay.

Ben volentieri (*very gladly, very willingly*) is generally used after the verb and it expresses interest and enthusiasm in doing something.

Vado **ben volentieri** a scuola.	*I go **very gladly** to school.*
Ti vedo molto **ben volentieri**.	*I am **very happy** to see you.*
	(*I see you **very willingly**.*)

Notice that **bene** drops the final **e** to become **ben** in front of **volentieri**.

Sentirsi di (*to feel like*) is used to express one's feeling to do or not to do something.

Ti senti di andare a sciare?	***Do you feel like** going skiing?*
Vi sentite di stare soli in casa?	***Do you feel like** staying at home alone?*

Non poterne più (*to be sick of, to be fed up with*) is used to express a feeling of frustration.

Non ne posso più dell'inverno.	*I am really **fed up** with winter.*
Non ne possiamo più di studiare.	*We are **fed up** with studying.*

Essere d'accordo (*to agree*) is used to express agreement.

Lei **è d'accordo** con me.	*She **agrees** with me.*
Siamo d'accordo, venite a cena da noi.	*We **agree**, you will come to dinner at our house.*

Below are additional phrases commonly used in everyday conversational Italian:

Fa attenzione!	*Pay attention!*
Fila via!	*Go away!*
Pover'uomo!	*Poor man!*
Smettila!	*Stop it! Knock it off!*
Stai zitto!	*Be quiet!*
Vattene!	*Go away!*

ESERCIZIO
14·1

Complete the following sentences with the appropriate expression, using the words in parentheses.

1. Vengo ben _____ con voi al cinema. (*very willingly*)

2. Stiamo _____ in casa questa sera. (*very willingly*)

3. Non mi _____ di spendere tutti quei soldi. (*to feel like*)

4. Io non ne _____ più di tutto quel chiasso. (*to be fed up*)

5. Io ne _____ più di tutte queste chiacchiere. (*to be fed up*)

6. Noi siamo _____ che ci vediamo questa sera. (*to agree*)

7. Io sono _____ con te per andare in gita. (*to agree*)

8. Vengo ben _____ con voi, non ne _____ più di stare in casa. (*very willingly, to be fed up*)

Idioms are phrases that acquire their meaning from an entire expression and cannot be translated word for word. In Italian, idioms are called **frasi idiomatiche** or **frasi fatte**.

Idioms are mostly used in one form, but some change in order to agree with the subject and verb as needed.

Quel ragazzo ha le mani bucate.	*That young man spends money without thinking.*
È bagnato dalla testa ai piedi.	*He is wet from head to toe.*
In bocca al lupo!	*Good luck!*

Following are some of the most commonly used Italian idioms:

A buon mercato	*Inexpensively*
A parte gli scherzi	*Seriously*
A sbaffo	*Without paying*
A tutti i costi	*At all cost*
Ad occhio e croce	*More or less*
Alla carlona	*Without any care*
Alle prime armi	*With no experience*
Aspetta e spera.	*Some things will never happen.*
Attenzione, pronti, via!	*Get on your mark, get set, go!*
Avere le mani bucate	*To spend without thinking*

Cadere dalle nuvole	*To fall from the clouds*
Dalla testa ai piedi	*From head to toe*
Dio li fa, poi li accompagna.	*God makes them, then mates them.*
È innamorato pazzo di lei.	*He is madly in love with her.*
Lui è al verde.	*He is short of cash.*
Meglio tardi che mai.	*Better late than never.*
Non me ne importa niente.	*It does not matter to me. I do not care at all.*
Ogni morte di Papa	*Once in a blue moon*
Per quanto ne sappia.	*As far as I know.*
Sono in un vero pasticcio!	*I am in a real fix!*
Testa o croce?	*Heads or tails?*

These are just a few of the hundreds of idioms in the Italian language. Try to learn as many as possible. By learning and using them, you will feel closer to native Italians and you will increase your ability to converse more richly.

ESERCIZIO
14·2

Write an original statement that would provoke the response given.

EXAMPLE: Non la vedo mai.

Viene ogni morte di Papa.

1. _____

   Vattene!

2. _____

   Non me ne importa niente.

3. _____

   Meglio tardi che mai.

4. _____

   Stai zitto!

5. _____

   Acqua in bocca!

6. _____

   Alle prime armi.

7. _____

   È a buon mercato.

8. _____

   Ha le mani bucate.

Reflexive verbs in special phrases

Some Italian expressions require a reflexive verb. Listed below are some examples that illustrate its use. You will notice that in the English translations the reflexive is not always used.

Arrangiati!	*Take care of it yourself!*
Ci sistemiamo nell'appartamento.	*We settle into the apartment.*
Deciditi una volta per sempre!	*Make up your mind once and for all!*
Mi accomodo nella poltrona.	*I make myself comfortable in the armchair.*
Mi spremo il cervello, ma non ricordo.	*I rack my brain, but I cannot remember.*
Muoviti!	*Hurry up!*
Non guastarti il sangue!	*Do not get mad!*
Non ti impicciare degli affari miei!	*It is none of your business!*
Non voglio cacciarmi in un pasticcio.	*I do not want to get into trouble.*
Si arrangia bene.	*He manages OK.*
Si comporta male.	*He behaves badly.*
Si è fatto male al ginocchio.	*He hurt his knee.*
Si rende conto dell'errore che ha fatto.	*He realizes the mistake he has made.*
Si trovano a loro agio con noi.	*They feel comfortable with us.*
Ti ricordi?	*Do you remember?*
Togliti di mezzo!	*Get out of the way!*

ESERCIZIO
14·3

Complete each sentence with the appropriate reflexive expression, using the words in parentheses.

1. Non voglio che portino i bambini a casa mia perchè si _____. (*behave badly*)

2. _____! Non voglio più vederti. (*go away*)

3. Se non vuoi che ti aiuti, _____. (*take care of it yourself*)

4. _____, ma non riesco a ricordare il suo nome. (*I rack my brain*)

5. Luisa è caduta e _____ al gomito. (*to get hurt*)

6. _____! Il treno parte! (*Hurry up!*)

7. Gli dico sempre di non _____ miei. (*to mind his own business*)

8. Mi _____ e le chiedo di sposarmi. (*settle into the apartment*)

Antonyms and contrasts

Antonyms are words that express opposite meanings. However, many words are not actually antonyms—they're not opposites of each other but rather contrasts. Both antonyms and contrasts are useful in creating interesting sentences. *Antonym* in Italian is **antonimo**:

> **sinistra** (*left*) ← **antonimo** → **destra** (*right*)

Verb antonyms

Following is a list of common antonyms and contrasts in verb form:

accendere/spegnere	*to turn on/to turn off*
amare/odiare	*to love/to hate*
arrivare/partire	*to arrive/to leave*
bere/morire di sete	*to drink/to die of thirst*
comprare/vendere	*to buy/to sell*
dare/prendere	*to give/to take*
essere orgoglioso/vergognarsi	*to be proud/to be ashamed*
giocare/lavorare	*to play/to work*
mandare/ricevere	*to send/to receive*
permettere/proibire	*to allow/to forbid*
ridere/piangere	*to laugh/to cry*
rompere/aggiustare	*to break/to repair*
salire/scendere	*to go up/to come down*
spingere/tirare	*to push/to pull*
venire/andare	*to come/to go*
vivere/morire	*to live/to die*

ESERCIZIO
15·1

Write a negative response to each of the following questions by using the antonym (contrasting verb) to the one used in the question.

EXAMPLE: Ami tu quel ragazzo?

No, affatto! Io lo odio.

1. Hai acceso la luce?

_____

2. Giochi a tennis venerdì?

_____

3. Eric ha rotto la sua racchetta da tennis?

_____

4. Avete comprato la casa?

_____

5. Hai riso al cinema?

_____

6. Franco ha aperto la porta?

_____

7. Hai bevuto la birra?

_____

8. Sono saliti sull'autobus i ragazzi?

_____

Noun antonyms

Other antonyms or contrasting pairs are nouns. Following is a list of some common noun antonyms:

acquisto/vendita	*buying/selling*
amore/odio	*love/hate*
caldo/freddo	*warm/cold*
apertura/chiusura	*opening/closing*
città/campagna	*city/country*
commedia/tragedia	*comedy/tragedy*
domanda/risposta	*question/answer*
entrata/uscita	*entry/exit*
felicità/tristezza	*happiness/sadness*
forza/debolezza	*strength/weakness*
giorno/notte	*day/night*
guerra/pace	*war/peace*
malattia/salute	*sickness/health*
marito/moglie	*husband/wife*
pianura/montagna	*plains/mountains*
prigionia/libertà	*imprisonment/freedom*
ragazzo/ragazza	*boy/girl*
ricchezza/povertà	*wealth/poverty*
salita/discesa	*ascent/descent*
uomo/donna	*man/woman*
vita/morte	*life/death*

Complete the following sentences using the appropriate antonyms.

1. Ti piacciono le commedie? No, io preferisco _____ .

2. Vedo l'uscita, ma dov'è _____ ?

3. Ha passato tanti anni in prigionia, ora si gode la _____ .

4. Dobbiamo godere la vita e aspettare la _____ .

5. Quando si ha una malattia si apprezza la _____ .

6. Molte novelle sono state scritte sull'amore e sull'_____ .

7. Per arrivare a casa sua in montagna bisogna prima fare una _____ e poi

   andare in _____ .

8. Il _____ è per lavorare e la _____ per dormire.

9. Alla televisione ci sono giochi con le _____ e le _____ .

10. La _____ porta distruzione e la _____ porta prosperità.

Adjective and adverb antonyms

There are many adjectives and adverbs that make antonyms or contrasting pairs.

affamato/sazio	hungry/satiated
asciutto/bagnato	dry/wet
bello/brutto	beautiful/ugly
buono/cattivo	good/bad
facile/difficile	easy/difficult
felice/infelice	happy/unhappy
freddo/caldo	cold/hot
grande/piccolo	big/small
interessante/noioso	interesting/boring
istruito/ignorante	educated/ignorant
leggero/pesante	light/heavy
lento/svelto	slow/fast
lungo/corto	long/short
magro/grasso	thin/fat
pigro/attivo	lazy/active
presto/tardi	early/late
pulito/sporco	clean/dirty
ricco/povero	rich/poor
scuro/chiaro	dark/light
semplice/complicato	simple/complicated
sorridente/serio	smiling/serious
stanco/riposato	tired/rested
trasparente/opaco	transparent/opaque

Using the adjectives given, write original sentences describing how someone or something is the opposite.

EXAMPLE: sorridente   *Lei non è una persona sorridente, ma è seria.*

1. lungo _____

2. pulito _____

3. felice _____

4. magro _____

5. interessante _____

6. leggero _____

7. facile _____

8. ricco _____

Passive voice

Verb constructions have two voices: active and passive. In the active voice the *subject* performs the action indicated by the verb and the *object* undergoes this action. The active voice emphasizes who is doing the action.

Io **guido** la macchina.	I **drive** the car.
Giovanni **compra** il giornale.	Giovanni **buys** the newspaper.

In the passive voice the *subject* undergoes the action. It emphasizes the fact, the action, or what has occurred. The performer, or agent, of the action is preceded by the preposition **da** (*by*) or its contractions: **dal, dallo, dalla, dai, dagli, dalle**. The active voice is almost always preferred in colloquial Italian. The passive voice is used in its place when one does not want to name or does not know the agent of the action.

subject + passive verb + da + agent

La finestra è chiusa da mia sorella.	*The window is being closed by my sister.*
La macchina **è guidata da** me.	*The car **is driven by** me.*
Il giornale **è comprato da** Giovanni.	*The newspaper **is bought by** Giovanni.*

An active sentence can be changed to passive only if the verb is transitive, that is, if it has a direct object. When this change occurs, the object of the active sentence becomes the subject of the passive one. The verb used is: ***essere* + the past participle** of the verb. The past participle in the passive sentence always agrees with the subject of the sentence.

subject + verb + object

Io mangio la mela.	*I eat the apple.*

subject + verb + da + agent

La mela è mangiata da me.	*The apple is eaten by me.*
La mia casa **è stata costruita** su una collina.	*My house **has been built** on a hill.*
Il presidente **è stato eletto** dalla popolazione.	*The president **was elected** by the people.*

Change the following sentences from the active into passive, using the words in parentheses.

1. Chi guarda il programma televisivo? (i bambini)

   _____

2. Chi gestisce questo bar? (Giovanni)

   _____

3. Chi compra la casa nuova? (mia figlia)

   _____

4. Chi scrive il libro? (il professore di italiano)

   _____

5. Chi legge il nuovo romanzo giallo? (gli studenti)

   _____

6. Chi costruisce questo bel palazzo? (un famoso architetto)

   _____

7. Chi fa il viaggio in Asia? (i miei amici)

   _____

8. Chi beve la birra? (Luigi)

   _____

Any tense can have a passive voice, for example:

Present
Molti giocattoli **sono dati** ai bambini per Natale.

*Many toys **are given** to children at Christmas.*

Future
Molti giocattoli **saranno dati** ai bambini per Natale.

*Many toys **will be given** to children at Christmas.*

Imperfect
Molti giocattoli **erano dati** ai bambini per Natale.

*Many toys **were given** to children at Christmas.*

Present perfect
Molti giocattoli **sono stati dati** ai bambini per Natale.

*Many toys **have been given** to children at Christmas.*

Pluperfect

Molti giocattoli **erano stati dati** ai bambini per Natale.

*Many toys **had been given** to children at Christmas.*

Conditional

Molti giocattoli **sarebbero dati** ai bambini per Natale.

*Many toys **would be given** to children at Christmas.*

Past conditional

Molti giocattoli **sarebbero stati dati** ai bambini per Natale.

*Many toys **would have been given** to children at Christmas.*

Venire with the passive voice

Instead of using the auxiliary verb **essere**, it is possible to use the verb **venire** to form the passive voice. **Venire** in the passive voice is used only with simple tenses, such as the present, imperfect, historical past, and future, and not with the compound tenses. If the agent performing the action is expressed after the verb, **da** precedes it.

subject + venire + past participle + da + agent

La casa viene imbiancata da suo padre.

The house is being painted by his father.

I cittadini **eleggono** il presidente.
→ Il presidente **viene eletto dai** cittadini.

*The citizens **elect** the president.*
*The president **is elected by the** people.*

Molti turisti **visitano** Firenze.
→ Firenze **viene visitata da** molti turisti.

*Many tourists **visit** Florence.*
*Florence **is visited by** many tourists.*

ESERCIZIO
16·2

*Rewrite the following questions in the passive using the verb **venire**.*

1. Chi prenota l'albergo?

   _____

2. Chi indirizza le lettere?

   _____

3. Chi interpreta il film?

   _____

4. Chi organizza la festa?

   _____

5. Chi invia questi pacchi?

   _____

6. Chi firma il documento?

   _____

7. Chi paga il conto?

_____

8. Chi prepara la cena?

_____

_____

ESERCIZIO
16·3

*Answer the questions in Esercizio 16-2 in the passive using the verb **venire** and the following suggestions.*

1. mio fratello

_____

2. segretaria

_____

3. Sofia Loren

_____

4. miei amici

_____

5. mamma

_____

6. notaio

_____

7. mio padre

_____

8. cuoca

_____

_____

Andare with the passive voice

It is also possible to use ***andare*** + **the past participle** to form the passive voice. This implies an obligation or necessity and is synonymous with **dover essere** (*must be, has to be*).

subject + andare + past participle + adverb

La casa va pulita spesso.	*The house has to be cleaned often.*
Il cane va portato fuori tutti i giorni.	*The dog **must be taken** out every day.*
I bambini vanno seguiti sempre.	*Children **have to** (**must**) **be followed** all the time.*

Using the words in parentheses, complete the following sentences with the correct form of **andare** + *the past participle.*

1. La televisione _____ quando hai finito di guardarla. (spegnere)

2. La strada _____ dopo che ha finito di nevicare. (spalare)

3. Il giornale _____ quando hai finito di leggerlo. (buttare)

4. I vetri _____ dopo la pioggia. (asciugare)

5. Il motore della macchina _____ ogni tre mesi. (controllare)

6. I bambini _____ il più possibile. (lodare)

7. I vecchi _____ quando sono in difficoltà. (aiutare)

8. I piatti _____ dopo che si sono usati. (lavare)

Si with the passive voice

The pronoun **si** is also used to create the passive voice with the third person of the active verb. This construction is called **si passivante**.

> **si + verb + direct object + complement of location**
>
> **Si vedono le oche nel laghetto.** — *The geese are seen in the small lake.*
>
> La domenica **non si lavora**. — *On Sunday, **one does not work**.*
> In Italia **si dà** troppa importanza alla moda. — *In Italy, too much importance **is given** to fashion.*

Sometimes you will see the use of the **si passivante** in newspaper advertisements, selling or renting signs, or newspaper articles. In this case, **si** is attached to the verb.

> **Affittasi** monolocale ristrutturato. — *Remodeled apartment for rent.*
> **Vendesi** casa con giardino. — *Home with garden for sale.*

When using the **si passivante**, it is important to remember transitive verbs agree in gender and number with the subject when they following **si**. If the verb is followed by another verb or an intransitive verb, agreement is not necessary.

> Abbiamo **visto molti musei**. — *We have **seen many museums**.*
> Si sono **visti molti musei**. — ***Many museums** have been **seen**.*
> **Dormiamo** per riposare. — *We **sleep** to rest.*
> **Si dorme** per riposare. — *One **sleeps** to rest.*

Rewrite the following sentences in the passive using the **si passivante**.

1. Lavoriamo per vivere.

   _____

2. Abbiamo lavorato tanti anni per avere un certo benessere.

   _____

3. Hanno piantato tanti fiori per avere un bel giardino.

   _____

4. Di notte vediamo tante stelle.

   _____

5. Porteremo tante cose in Italia per le nostre nipoti.

   _____

6. In America viviamo bene.

   _____

7. In questa casa parliamo solo italiano.

   _____

8. Negli aeroporti vediamo tante cose strane.

   _____

Subjunctive mood

The subjunctive is used to express wishes, doubts, possibilities, and opinions, unlike the indicative, which expresses facts and conveys information. In contemporary Italian, there is a tendency to replace the subjunctive with the indicative, but a good speaker or writer does not let this happen. The subjunctive has four tenses: two simple (present and imperfect) and two compound (past and pluperfect). The subjunctive is generally used in dependent clauses introduced by **che**.

main clause + che + subjunctive tense

Credo che tu venga.	*I think that you will come.*

Present subjunctive

Assuming that you have already studied the subjunctive, this chapter will not dwell so much on its conjugation as on its use, which is rather complex. The present subjunctive expresses a present action with respect to the main verb. It is used in dependent clauses where there is a present or a future tense in the main clause.

present/future indicative + che + present subjunctive

Credi che io possa venire da te?	*Do you think that I can come to your house?*
Penso che **sia** una scelta giusta.	*I think **it is** the right choice.*
Penseranno che **tu sia** una persona importante.	*They will think that **you are** an important person.*
Il dottore vuole che **io mangi** molta frutta.	*The doctor wants **me to eat** a lot of fruit.*
Mi sembra che **tu abbia** molta pazienza.	*It seems to me that **you have** a lot of patience.*
Lei crede che **voi siate** sempre affamati.	*She believes that **you are** always hungry.*

Some important facts to keep in mind about the present subjunctive:

◆ It is necessary to use the subject pronoun with the **io**, **tu**, **lui/lei** verb forms, since the endings are often the same.
◆ In addition to the regular verbs in the third conjugation forms, there are those conjugated with **-isc**.
◆ In the first conjugation, with verbs ending in **-care** and **-gare**, in order to keep the hard sound of **c** and **g** before the **i**, it is necessary to add **h** before all endings.

Bisogna che **voi paghiate** il conto.   *It is necessary that **you pay** the bill.*

◆ The verbs ending in **-ciare** and **-giare** drop the **-i** of the endings.

Credo che il film **cominci** fra un'ora.   *I think that the movie **is going to start** in one hour.*

Mi sembra che **mangiate** troppo.   *It seems to me that **you are eating** too much.*

ESERCIZIO
17·1

Complete the following sentences with the correct forms of the verbs in parentheses.

1. Tu credi che io _____ in tempo? (fare)

2. La professoressa vuole che tu _____ più attento. (stare)

3. È ora che io _____ di casa e _____ a lavorare. (uscire, andare)

4. Spero che lo spettacolo _____ divertente. (essere)

5. Penso che lui _____ domani pomeriggio. (arrivare)

6. Spero che non _____ troppo freddo. (fare)

7. Credo che voi _____ a casa. (ritornare)

8. Pensa che noi _____ poco. (dormire)

When the subject of the main sentence and the dependent sentence is the same, the infinitive is used instead of the subjunctive. The preposition **di** precedes the infinitive.

present indicative + di + infinitive

Crede di sapere tutto.   *He thinks he knows everything.*

Past subjunctive

The past subjunctive expresses a past action with respect to the main verb. It is used in dependent clauses when there is a future or a present tense in the main clause. It is formed by the present subjunctive of the auxiliary **essere** or **avere** followed by the past participle of the verb.

present indicative + che + past subjunctive

Sono felice che siate ritornati.	*I am happy that you returned.*
Sono contento che tu mi **abbia chiamato**.	*I am happy that you **called** me.*
È impossibile che lui **abbia comprato** una casa.	*It is impossible that **he bought** a house.*
Mi dispiace che loro **siano** già **partiti**.	*I am sorry that they **have** already **left**.*
Penserà che tu **abbia voluto** vederlo.	*He will think that you **wanted** to see him.*

ESERCIZIO 17·2

Complete the following sentences with the past subjunctive of the verbs in parentheses.

1. Tutti credono che io _____ il dolce. (fare)

2. Penso che loro _____ la lotteria. (vincere)

3. Luisa è la persona più colta che io _____. (conoscere)

4. Lei crede che voi _____ tutto. (mangiare)

5. Credo che quella donna _____ i suoi figli. (trascurare)

6. Penso che voi _____ un bel libro. (leggere)

7. Mi sembra che ieri _____. (nevicare)

8. Penso che voi _____ la mia lettera. (ricevere)

Imperfect subjunctive

The imperfect subjunctive is used in the dependent clause when the past tense is used in the main clause. It expresses a thought, a belief, or a hope in the past.

subject + imperfect indicative + che + imperfect subjunctive

Io pensavo che tu venissi da me.	*I thought you would come to my house.*
Luisa voleva che io par**lassi** con sua madre.	***Luisa wanted** me **to speak** to her mother.*
Pensavo che tu ven**dessi** la tua casa.	***I thought you were selling** your home.*
Giovanni credeva che voi part**iste** con il treno.	***Giovanni thought you would leave** by train.*

The imperfect subjunctive is also used in a dependent clause when the present conditional appears in the main clause. It expresses a wish that may or may not be realized in the present.

verb in the conditional + che + imperfect subjunctive

Vorrei che tu parlassi di più.	*I wish you talked more.*
Vorrei che tu **scrivessi** a tua madre.	***I would like** you **to write** to your mother.*
Mi piacerebbe che lei **studiasse** medicina.	***I would like** her **to study** medicine.*
Vorrebbero che io **comprassi** una casa.	***They would like** me **to buy** a house.*

Complete the following sentences with the imperfect subjunctive of the verbs in parentheses.

1. Tutti volevano che io _____ il dolce. (fare)

2. Desideravo che loro _____ la lotteria. (vincere)

3. Teresa era l'amica più cara che io _____. (avere)

4. Lei credeva che voi _____ tutto. (mangiare)

5. Mi sembrava che quella donna _____ i suoi figli. (trascurare)

6. Pensavo che vi _____ un bel libro. (piacere)

7. Volevano che _____ molto. (nevicare)

8. Pensavate che io _____ la vostra lettera prima di partire. (ricevere)

Pluperfect subjunctive

The pluperfect subjunctive is used to express a desire, a hope, or a thought that has not been realized in the past. It is also used in dependent clauses when the verb of the main clause is in the past.

The pluperfect subjunctive is formed with the imperfect subjunctive of the auxiliary verbs **essere** or **avere** and the past participle of the verb showing the action. Because the first and the second person singular have the same endings, it is preferable to use the subject pronouns to avoid ambiguity.

imperfect + che + pluperfect subjunctive

Pensavo che tu avessi dormito bene.	*I thought you had slept well.*
Credevo che tu **avessi parlato** con Maria.	*I believed that you **had spoken** with Maria.*
Non sapevo che lei **avesse comprato** la casa.	*I did not know that she **had bought** a house.*
Noi pensavamo che voi **foste** già **partiti**.	*We thought that you **had** already **left**.*
Pensavamo che voi non **foste arrivati**.	*We thought that you **had** not **arrived**.*

Complete the following sentences with the pluperfect subjunctive of the verbs in parentheses.

1. Pensavamo che Mario _____ di più per gli esami. (studiare)

2. Temevamo che voi non _____ il biglietto. (fare)

3. Io avrei voluto che voi _____ con me in Africa. (venire)

4. Pensavo che loro _____ già _____ in Florida. (andare)

5. Pensavate che _____ con il treno? (io-arrivare)

6. Non sapevo che tu _____ la tua macchina. (vendere)

7. Non credevo che tu _____ senza salutare. (partire)

8. Mi sembrava che a Paolo non _____ il ristorante. (piacere)

Uses of the subjunctive in independent clauses

In a main or independent clause, the subjunctive may express:

- An exhortation or an order, instead of using the formal imperative. The present subjunctive is used in this instance.

Abbia pazienza!	**Be** patient!
Stia zitto!	**Be** quiet!

- The giving of permission or an invitation

Venga pure a trovarci!	Of course, **come** and see us!

- A doubt. The present or past subjunctive is used in this case.

Non è venuto! Che **si sia dimenticato**?	He did not come! Could it be possible **that he forgot**?
Luisa non ha chiamato! Che **abbia perso** il numero di telefono?	Luisa did not call! Could **she have lost** our phone number?

- A wish, a desire, or a prohibition

Magari **vincessi**!	If only **I won**!
Dio vi **benedica**!	God **bless** you!
Che non **succeda** mai più!	May it never **happen** again!

- An exclamation

Vedessi come è bello il lago di Como!	**If you could only see** how beautiful Lake Como is!
Sapessi che paura ho degli esami!	**If you only knew** how scared I am of finals!

ESERCIZIO
17·5

Using the verbs in parentheses, complete the following sentences with the correct forms of the subjunctive.

1. Tu _____ come sono belle le Hawaii! (sapere)

2. Tu _____ quanta gente c'è in piazza! (vedere)

3. (Voi) _____ pazienza con i vecchi! (avere)

4. _____ signora! Il dottore viene subito. (accomodarsi)

5. Loro _____ zitti! (stare)

6. _____ agli affari suoi! (pensare)

7. Che Dio vi _____! (aiutare)

8. Magari _____! (io-dormire)

Uses of the subjunctive in dependent clauses

It is necessary to use the subjunctive after the following subordinating conjunctions and expressions:

a condizione che	*on condition that*	nonostante	*despite*
affinchè	*so that*	perchè	*so that*
appena che	*as soon as*	prima che	*before*
benchè	*although*	purchè	*provided that*
come se	*as if*	sebbene	*although*
dopo che	*after*	senza che	*without*
nel caso che	*on condition that*		

Lo dico **affinchè** tutti lo sappiano.   *I am saying it, **so that** everybody knows.*
Vado al cinema, **benchè** piova.   *I am going to the movies, **although** it is raining.*
Abbiamo saputo la notizia **prima che** lo   *We knew the news **before** others found out.*
    sapessero gli altri.

The subjunctive is also used with these indefinite pronouns and adjectives:

chiunque	*whoever*	qualunque	*any*
dovunque	*wherever*	qualunque cosa	*whatever*
qualsiasi	*any*		

Chiunque lo voglia, potrà prendere lezioni   ***Whoever** wants to can take skiing lessons.*
    di sci.
Dovunque siate, verrò a visitarvi.   ***Wherever** you are, I will visit you.*
Qualunque cosa vogliano, gliela   ***Anything** they want, we will buy it for her.*
    compriamo.

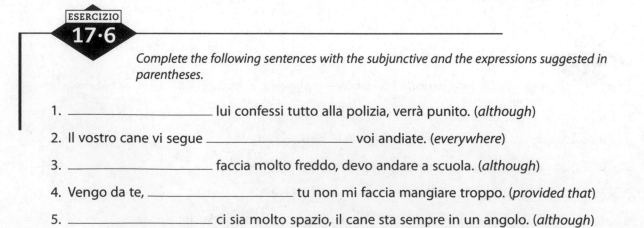

ESERCIZIO
17·6

Complete the following sentences with the subjunctive and the expressions suggested in parentheses.

1. _____ lui confessi tutto alla polizia, verrà punito. (*although*)

2. Il vostro cane vi segue _____ voi andiate. (*everywhere*)

3. _____ faccia molto freddo, devo andare a scuola. (*although*)

4. Vengo da te, _____ tu non mi faccia mangiare troppo. (*provided that*)

5. _____ ci sia molto spazio, il cane sta sempre in un angolo. (*although*)

6. _____ voi abbiate detto niente, hanno scoperto il modo di aprire la porta. (*though*)

7. _____ loro venissero, abbiamo pulito la casa. (*before*)

8. Abbiamo chiuso la porta _____ nessuno senta quel che diciamo. (*so that*)

The subjunctive is used after impersonal expressions. These expressions appear only in the third person singular and they are formed by using the verb **essere** + **an adjective**:

essere + **adverb** + **che** + **subjunctive** + **object**

È impossibile che tu abbia finito il tuo lavoro.　　*It is impossible that you finished your work.*

È bene/male che	*It is good/bad that*	È necessario che	*It is necessary that*
È giusto che	*It is fair that*	È opportuno che	*It is convenient that*
È impossibile che	*It is impossible that*	È possibile che	*It is possible that*
È meglio che	*It is better that*	È utile/inutile che	*It is useful/useless that*

È meglio che voi **aspettiate** l'autobus.　　*It is better that you wait for the bus.*
È necessario che lui **vada** dal dottore.　　*It is necessary that he go to the doctor.*
È giusto che lo **paghino** per il suo lavoro.　　*It is right that they pay him for his work.*

The subjunctive is also used with verbs that express necessity. The verbs in this instance are always used in the third person singular.

avere bisogno	*to need*	convenire	*to be worth*
bastare	*to be enough*	occorrere	*to need*
bisognare	*to be necessary*	valere la pena	*to be worth*

Bisogna che voi **andiate** dal calzolaio.　　*It is necessary that you go to the shoemaker.*
Occorre che lei **parli** con il padrone.　　*It is necessary that she speak with the landlord.*

Vale la pena che tu **compri** una macchina usata.　　*It is worth it for you to buy a used car.*

ESERCIZIO
17·7

Complete the following sentences with the appropriate forms of the subjunctive, using the verbs in parentheses.

1. È impossibile che voi _____ a ballare bene. (imparare)

2. Era impossibile che tu _____ a ballare bene. (imparare)

3. È meglio che voi _____ lontano da me. (stare)

4. Sarebbe stato meglio che lei _____ lontano da lui. (stare)

5. È bene che noi _____ le istruzioni prima di cominciare. (ascoltare)

6. Non è giusto che il professore mi _____ un brutto voto. (dare)

7. Bisogna che tu _____ tua sorella. (chiamare)

8. È necessario che lui _____ a letto la bambina. (mettere)

The subjunctive is used after verbs that express a command, a wish, hope, fear, permission, emotion, doubt, expectation, or uncertainty.

aspettare	*to wait*	desiderare	*to wish*
aspettarsi	*to expect*	dubitare	*to doubt*
augurarsi	*to wish*	essere contento	*to be happy*
avere paura	*to be afraid*	ordinare	*to order*
consentire	*to allow*	sperare	*to hope*
credere	*to believe*	temere	*to fear*

Ci **auguriamo** che tutto vada bene.   *We **hope** that everything goes well.*
Spero che voi mi telefoniate.   *I **hope** that you will call me.*
Desidero che tu rimanga da me.   *I **wish** that you would stay at my house.*

ESERCIZIO
17·8

Complete the following sentences with the appropriate forms of the subjunctive.

1. Bisogna che _____.

2. Spero che _____.

3. Tutti pensano che _____.

4. Temiamo che _____.

5. Ho paura che _____.

6. Mi auguro che _____.

7. Aspetto che _____.

8. Sono contenti che _____.

Subjunctive after the conjunction *se*

The subjunctive is used after the conjunction **se** (*if*) if the clause that follows expresses a condition that cannot be true, or if it refers to something that is impossible to realize. The example sentences shown below are the same in meaning, except the first expresses a wish that cannot be realized in the present while the second expresses the same wish that could not be realized in the past.

se + imperfect subjunctive + present conditional

Se potessi viaggerei con te.   *If I could, I would travel with you.*

se + pluperfect subjunctive + past conditional

Se avessi potuto avrei viaggiato con te.   *If I had been able, I would have traveled with you.*

Se avessi i soldi, comprerei una casa in Italia.	*If I had the money, I would buy a home in Italy.*
Se me l'avessi detto, ti avrei aspettato.	*If you had told me, I would have waited for you.*

When the condition being expressed is a known fact the **se** clause is followed by a tense in the indicative instead of the subjunctive.

Se studi, impari.	*If you study, you will learn.*
Se hai sete, bevi l'acqua.	*If you are thirsty, drink water.*

Subjunctive in relative clauses

The subjunctive is used in relative clauses introduced by negatives such as **niente, nessuno**, or **non c'è**.

Non c'é niente che mi sorprenda.	*There is nothing that will surprise me.*
Non trovo nessuno che mi possa aiutare.	*I cannot find anybody who can help me.*

It is also used with a relative clause introduced by an adjective or a superlative such as **primo**, **supremo, ultimo**, or **unico**.

Luisa è l'**unica amica** che mi abbia scritto.	*Luisa is the **only friend** who wrote to me.*
Tu sei la persona **più gentile** che io conosca.	*You are the **kindest** person (whom) I know.*

The indefinite expressions **uno**, **una**, **qualcuno**, and **qualcosa** can be used with the subjunctive.

Cerco **uno che** sappia l'inglese.	*I am looking for **someone who** knows English.*
Hai **qualcosa** che mi faccia passare il mal di testa?	*Do you have **anything** that will help get rid of my headache?*

ESERCIZIO
17·9

Complete the following sentences with the appropriate forms of the subjunctive, using the verbs in parentheses.

1. Se _____, sarei venuto. (potere)

2. Se mi _____, sarei venuta ad aiutarti. (chiamare)

3. Se _____ i soldi, comprerei una macchina a mio figlio. (avere)

4. Se _____ i soldi, avrei comprato una macchina a mio figlio. (avere)

5. Se voi _____, imparereste. (studiare)

6. Se loro _____, avebbero imparato. (studiare)

7. Non credo ci sia nessuno che _____ l'arabo. (parlare)

8. Non c'è niente che mi _____. (piacere)

Punctuation

Punctuation is the only instrument we have to give written language the various nuances and tones that we give spoken language. The entire punctuation system is made up of signs (period, comma, etc.) that reproduce voice intonation, and by graphic signs (parentheses, asterisk, etc.) that help clarify the written text. Italian uses the same punctuation marks as English, although sometimes they are used in a different way, so it is important to familiarize yourself with their usage.

Period

The **period** is used to mark the end of a declarative sentence and indicates a prolonged pause of the voice. The word coming after the period must be written with a capital letter, and when a paragraph is completed it is necessary to start the next one on a different line.

La mamma è stanca.	*Mother is tired.*
I bambini giocano nel parco.	*The children play in the park.*
Domani non vado a scuola.	*Tomorrow I will not go to school.*

The period is also used with abbreviations and acronyms.

B.O.T.	Buoni Ordinari del Tesoro (*Treasury Bill*)
Dott.	dottore (*doctor*)
FF.SS.	Ferrovie dello Stato (*State-owned Railway*)
Sig.	signore (*mister*)
U.S.A.	United States of America

Unlike in English where a comma is used, in Italian a period separates the elements of a date. In Italian, the day precedes the month in dates.

11 gennaio 2009   →   11. 01. 2009

When writing numbers, either a period or a space may be used to separate every three digits, where a comma would be used in English. (The comma with Italian numbers indicates decimals.)

1.000 *or* 1 000	*1,000*
1.000.000 *or* 1 000 000	*1,000,000*

Comma

A **comma** separates the clauses in a sentence, the words forming a list, and the adjectives following an adverb.

Se questo non è sufficientemente chiaro, potrai telefonare.	*If this is not very clear, you may call.*
Unite la cipolla, il pepe, il sale, e un po' d'acqua.	*Add the onion, pepper, salt, and some water.*

In Italian the comma also:

- Signals a vocative (a change in form, language, word order, or intonation that indicates the one being addressed)

Ragazzi, sbrigatevi!	*Boys, hurry up!*
Luigi, non farlo!	*Luigi, do not do that!*
Abbi pietà, O Signore!	*Have mercy, O Lord!*

- Indicates a pause in the main sentence

Ci vedremo, forse domani mattina.	*We will see each other, maybe tomorrow.*
È venuto anche Davide, il fratello di Antonio.	*David, Anthony's brother, came too.*

- Comes before the conjunctions **ma**, **anzi**, **però**, **invece**, **tuttavia**, **benchè**, **se**, **sebbene**, and **mentre**

Mi piace la musica, ma non amo il jazz.	*I like music, but I do not love jazz.*
Ti aiuterò, benchè tu non lo meriti.	*I will help you, even if you do not deserve it.*

- Appears after **sì**, **no**, and **bene**

Sì, mi fa piacere vederti.	*Yes, I will be happy to see you.*
No, non posso andare al cinema.	*No, I cannot go to the movies.*

- Separates sentences in order to avoid the use of the conjunction **e**

Il giocoliere venne in pista, prese dei cerchi, cominciò a lanciarli in alto.	*The juggler came on the scene, took some hoops, started throwing them up in the air.*
L'aereo cadde nel fiume, gli elicotteri di sostegno arrivarono, la gente fu salvata.	*The plane crashed in the river, the rescue helicopters arrived, the passengers were saved.*

- Emphasizes the end of a speech with one of the many conclusion connectives such as **quindi**, **infatti**, **dunque**, **per finire**, **concludendo**, and **riassumendo**

Per finire, dico che è ora di cambiare!	*To finish, I say it is time to change!*
Infatti, nessuno ha capito niente.	*In fact, nobody has understood a thing.*

- Separates hours from minutes

La banca apre alle 8,30 e chiude alle 12,30.	*The bank will open at 8:30 and close at 12:30.*

The comma, more than any other punctuation mark, is used in a free, subjective way. However, there are some instances when the comma **cannot** be used:

♦ Before **nè**, **o**, or **e** when used between two nouns, adjectives, or pronouns

Non mangio i dolci **nè** la frutta.   *I do not eat sweets or fruit.*
Maria **e** Luigi vengono da me.   *Maria and Luigi will come to my house.*
Luisa è bella **e** intelligente.   *Luisa is beautiful and intelligent.*

♦ Between the subject and the verb

Fabio legge.   *Fabio is reading.*

♦ Between the verb and the first direct object in a sentence

Ho comprato la frutta, la verdure,   *I bought fruit, vegetables, and meat.*
   e la carne.

ESERCIZIO
18·1

Add the correct punctuation to the following sentences.

1. Il Sig Fortina non si è presentato per l'appuntamento

2. Il film che abbiamo visto insieme ha vinto l'Oscar

3. Maria ha trenta anni vive sola in una grande città

4. No non vengo a casa tua domani

5. Dunque per finire dico che bisogna parlare chiaramente

6. Vorrei vedere le chiese i musei e i parchi di Roma

7. Mi piace viaggiare ma ho paura di viaggiare in aereo

8. È venuto anche Luigi lo zio di Marco

Semicolon

A **semicolon** separates the parts of a clause with a shorter pause than that of a period, but more marked than that of a comma.

Pietro guardava la televisione con   *Peter was watching TV intently; Michele*
   interesse; Michele leggeva un libro;   *was reading a book; Maria was ironing in*
   Maria stirava in cucina.   *the kitchen.*

Other punctuation marks

A **colon** marks a brief pause and has a very definite function. It is used to introduce direct speech, a list of things, an explanation, or an example. Notice the difference between Italian and English when using the colon:

Disse: "Mi piace il mare".	*He said, "I like the sea."*
Ho mangiato: una mela, due mandarini, e tante noci.	*I ate an apple, two tangerines, and many nuts.*
Te l'ho già detto: "Non mi piace come ti comporti!"	*I have already told you, "I do not like your behavior!"*
Per esempio: due kiwi corrispondono a due mandarini per quantità di vitamina C.	*For example, two kiwis correspond to two tangerines in the amount of vitamin C.*

A **question mark** is used in direct questions or in expressions of doubt and incredulity.

Come vanno le cose?	*How are things going?*
Ma non dirai sul serio?	*You aren't speaking seriously?*

An **exclamation point** marks the end of a sentence expressing wonder, surprise, a request, a wish, an order, sorrow, or an invocation.

Che meraviglia la luna stasera!	*What a marvelous moon tonight!*
Come vorrei andare in Italia!	*How badly I want to go to Italy!*
Che peccato!	*What a pity!*

An **ellipsis** (...) indicates that speech is left unfinished. Italian uses a fixed number of three dots followed by a space to leave a sentence unfinished, whereas English uses three dots with a space around each dot (. . .).

Non vorrei dire, ma...	*I do not want to say anything, but . . .*
Mi ha detto: "Non fare commenti su..."	*She said to me, "Do not make any comments about . . ."*

ESERCIZIO 18·2

Rewrite the following sentences adding the proper punctuation marks.

1. Chi sono quelle persone

_____

2. No certo

_____

3. Dunque quel ragazzo è un pittore

_____

4. Dove vai vado all'aeroporto

_____

5. Quanta gente c'è per la strada Dove vanno

_____

6. Il mio lavoro è noioso poco interessante statico e facile

_____

7. Mia sorella disse mi piacerebbe andare a sciare ma non c'è abbastanza neve

_____

8. Io studio tanto ma non ricordo niente

_____

Graphic marks

Graphic marks help clarify written text and, thus, enable you to more clearly express yourself in writing.

- **Quotation marks** are used for direct speech, quotations, and the titles of books, newspapers, and magazines.

Maria chiese: "Come stai?"	*Maria asked, "How are you?"*
Come disse Galileo: "Eppur si muove".	*As Galileo said, "But it is moving."*
Ho letto: "L'Inferno", di Dante Alighieri.	*I read* The Inferno *by Dante Alighieri.*

- **Dashes** can replace quotation marks in direct speech. They are interchangeable. However, quotation marks are more common. This is not the case in English where dashes cannot replace quotation marks.

—Come stai?—chiese l'uomo.	*"How are you?" the man asked.*

- **Hyphens** mark a new line. In Italian, as in English, if one cannot finish writing a word on a line and needs to go to the next line, the word can be divided. Before going to a new line the hyphen is put at the end of the line next to the word that cannot be completed. Hyphens are also used between two words that make up a unit.

La partita **Inter–Milan**	*The **Inter–Milan** match*
Il volo **Francoforte–Roma**	*The **Frankfurt–Rome** flight*

- **Parentheses** are used to give an explanation or to make an example within a sentence.

Marco si alzò presto (dorme sempre fino a tardi) e decise di partire.	*Marco got up early (he always gets up late) and decided to leave.*
La terrazza (o meglio la veranda) di casa mia è molto grande.	*The deck (or rather the veranda) at my house is very large.*

- An **asterisk** (*) indicates a note at the foot of the page should an explanation, a name, or a translation need to be added. Three asterisks in succession (***) indicate a proper noun that one does not want to mention.

La ragazza era la figlia del Ministro***.	*The girl was the daughter of the Minister ***.*

- A **slash**, also called a forward slash (a name possibly familiar to you from using the Internet), indicates a choice of words or an alternative to a word.

scienze politiche e/o economiche	*political and/or economic science*

Write a complete sentence for each of the following punctuation marks: a colon, a question mark, an exclamation mark, quotation marks, an ellipsis, three asterisks, parentheses, and a hyphen.

1. _____

2. _____

3. _____

4. _____

5. _____

6. _____

7. _____

8. _____

Elision

An **elision** is used to make a smooth transition from one word to the next. It involves the elimination of the final vowel of a word before another word beginning with a vowel. In place of the dropped vowel, an apostrophe is used. The vowel pronunciation and stressing does not change.

lo amico → **l'**amico	*the friend*
la anima → **l'**anima	*the soul*

An elision is **mandatory** with:

◆ The definite articles **lo** and **la** and the compound prepositions formed with them

all'amico	*to the friend*
dell'uomo	*of the man*
l'uomo	*the man*
l'uva	*the grapes*

◆ The adverb **ci** before the forms of **essere** that begin with **e**

ci è → **c'**è	*there is*
ci erano → **c'**erano	*there were*

◆ The adjectives **bello/a, santo/a**

bello esempio → **bell'**esempio	*good example*
santo Andrea → **sant'**Andrea	*Saint Andrew*

◆ The demonstrative adjective **quello/a**

quello anello → **quell'**anello	*that ring*

◆ Some common expressions

tutt'altro	*on the contrary*
l'altr'anno	*last year*
tutt'al più	*at the most*
a quattr'occhi	*in private*

An elision is **optional** with:

◆ The pronouns **mi**, **ti**, **ci**, **si**, **vi**, and **ne**

mi interessa → **m'**interessa	*it interests me*
ti invito → **t'**invito	*I will invite you*

◆ The conjunction **anche** (*also, too*) followed by a subject pronoun

anche io → **anch'**io	*me too*

◆ The preposition **di**

di ottobre → **d'**ottobre	*in October*

◆ The adjective **grande** (*big*)

un grande uomo → un **grand'**uomo	*a great man*

The elision is **never** used when it would change the pronunciation of a word.

Ci is not elided before a word that starts with the vowels **a**, **o**, **u**: **ci amiamo** and not **c'amiamo**.

Da is elided only with the following expressions: **d'ora in avanti** (*from now on*), **d'ora in poi** (*from now on*), **d'altronde** (*on the other hand*), and **d'altra parte** (*then again, on the other hand*); otherwise, there could be some confusion with the preposition **di**.

D'ora in avanti, dovremo parlare in inglese.	***From now on**, we must speak English.*
D'altronde, se non vanno d'accordo, è meglio così.	***On the other hand**, if they cannot get along, it is better this way.*

The personal pronouns **le** and **li** are never elided: **le osserva** (*he observes them*) and not **l'osserva**; **li ama** (*he loves them*) and not **l'ama**; otherwise, it would be understood as being the singular form. (**L'osserva** would translate as *he/she observes him/her* and **l'ama** would be *he/she loves him/her*.)

Lui **le osserva** tutti i giorni.	*He observes them every day.*
Lui **l'osserva** dalla finestra.	*He observes him/her from the window.*

The articles and compound prepositions that come before words starting with **i** followed by another vowel are never elided: **lo iodio** (*the iodine*), **la iena** (*the hyena*).

La iena vive in Africa.	*The hyena lives in Africa.*
Metti il cibo nella gabbia **della iena**.	*Put the food in **the hyena's** cage.*

Rewrite each sentence, eliding the words that need an apostrophe.

1. La amica di mia mamma è molto simpatica. _____

2. Quello oggetto in vetrina è molto bello. _____

3. Vorrei parlargli a quattro occhi. _____

4. Non la ho ascoltata perchè chiacchieravo. _____

5. Non hai dato un bello esempio ai tuoi figli. _____

6. Luisa ha cercato di seguire le istruzioni alla bello e meglio. _____

7. La alunna non ha finito l'esame. _____

8. Lei compra la oca al supermercato. _____

Dropping a vowel or final syllable

Dropping a vowel or the final syllable of a word coming before a word starting with a consonant is common in Italian. This, too, is done to avoid an awkward and unpleasant sound in speaking. Notice that in the following cases the final vowel is omitted, but no apostrophe is used: **bel tipo** (*nice man*) and not **bello tipo**; **Buon Anno** (*Happy New Year*) and not **Buono Anno**; **mar Tirreno** (*Tyrrhenian Sea*) and not **mare Tirreno**.

The dropping of the final vowel or syllable is **mandatory** with:

◆ **Uno** and its compounds (**alcuno, ciascuno, nessuno**): **un amico** (*a friend*), **un leone** (*a lion*), **ciascun alunno** (*each student*), and **nessun gioco** (*no game*).

> Carlo è **un buon** amico.   *Carlo is **a good** friend.*
> Non c'è **nessun** posto.   *There is **no** place.*

◆ **Buono** followed by a word starting with a vowel or a consonant, for example, **buon uomo, buon gelato. Buono** with its final **o** is used at the end of a sentence or in front of words that start with **s** + **a consonant**.

> Questo è un dolce **buono.**   *This is a **good** cake.*
> Luigi è un **buono** studente.   *Luigi is a **good** student.*
> Vorrei un **buon** gelato alla nocciola.   *I would like a **good** hazelnut ice cream.*

◆ **Bello, santo,** and **quello** before nouns that would require the definite article **il**: **un bel libro, quel turista, san Giovanni,** etc.

> **Quel turista** non sa dove andare.   ***That tourist*** *does not know where to go.*
> Vorrei comprarmi **un bel libro** in Italia.   *I would like to buy **a good book** in Italy.*

◆ Commonly used words, such as **signore, professore, dottore,** and **ingegnere,** before a proper noun, for example, **il professor Corbetti, il dottor Bianchi, l'ingegner Carducci**

Il **professor Corbetti** è molto bravo.	*Professor Corbetti is very good.*
Oggi vado **dal dottor Bianchi** per una visita.	*Today I will go **to Dr. Bianchi** for a checkup.*

◆ A few words, such as **amore, bene, fiore, fine, fino**, and **male**, used in special expressions, including **amor mio** (*my love*), **ben fatto** (*well done*), **fior di panna** (*whipping cream*), **in fin dei conti** (*at the end*), **fin lì** (*up to there*), and **mal di mare** (*seasick*)

Questo lavoro è stato **ben fatto**.	*This job was **well done**.*
Quando vado in barca mi viene il **mal di mare**.	*When I go on a boat, I get seasick.*

Dropping the final vowel or syllable is **optional** with the words **grande, ora, ancora, allora**, and **talora**.

Non so **ancor** niente.	*I do not know anything **yet**.*
Avevo una **gran** paura.	*I was **really** scared.*

Do not drop the final vowel or syllable with plural words such as **buone intenzioni** (*good intentions*) or **quelle amicizie** (*those friendships*).

Quell'uomo non aveva **buone intenzioni**.	*That man did not have **good intentions**.*
Non mantenere **quelle amicizie**.	*Do not keep **those friendships**.*

Finally, **do not** drop the final vowel or syllable before words that begin with **z, gn, ps, x, s + a consonant**.

L'arpa è **uno strumento** interessante.	*The harp is **an interesting** musical instrument.*
Quello zaino è molto pesante.	***That backpack** is very heavy.*

Apocope is a special form of dropping the final vowel or syllable. In this case, the vowel or syllable is dropped independently from the word that follows and an apostrophe is used. (A word space remains after the apostrophe.) The most common cases of apocope are some verbs in the imperative form and a few other words, mostly deriving from dialectal use.

Imperatives	Other cases
dai → **da'**	bene → **be'**
dici → **di'**	casa → **ca'**
fai → **fa'**	modo → **mo'**
stai → **sta'**	poco → **po'**
vai → **va'**	tieni → **te'**
prendi → **to'**	
vedi → **ve'**	

Te' and **to'** are mostly used in place of **tieni** and **prendi** in colloquial Italian. Sometimes they are both used in the same sentence.

Te', tieni la corda!	*Hold the rope!*
To', prendi un biscotto!	*Take a cookie!*

Rewrite the following phrases, dropping the final vowel or syllable as appropriate.

1. un poco di pane _____

2. ciascuno alunno _____

3. buono anno _____

4. non date nessuno consiglio _____

5. dottore Gavozzi _____

6. grande serata _____

7. santa Anna _____

8. ancora niente _____

9. bene fatto _____

10. buono giorno _____

Complete the following sentences with the appropriate forms of apocopation.

1. Per favore, _____ il pane alle oche. (dare)

2. Oggi _____ a casa. (stare)

3. _____ fuori a giocare! (andare)

4. _____ , questi biscotti. (prendere)

5. Va _____ , ti chiamerò appena arrivo a casa. (bene)

6. Ma _____ che bella ragazza è diventata! (vedere)

7. _____ quel che vuoi, ma nessuno ascolta. (dire)

8. Vorremmo un _____ di pace e tranquillità. (poco)

Letter writing

19

There are some basic differences between letter writing in English and in Italian. Understanding these differences will not only help you get your point across better but will make your writing more interesting for the reader.

Address

When addressing an envelope in Italian, the order of the lines is slightly different from the English format. Often in English the **title** of the addressee, such as Mr., Mrs., or Ms., is left out, especially if the letter is addressed to a friend or relative and if the letter is casual. In Italian, however, even when addressing an envelope to a friend or relative, it is very rare to omit the person's title before the name.

> Gent.mo Sig. (*Very Kind Mr.*)
> Gili Riccardo
> Via Sant'Isaia, 23
> 40134 Bologna
> Italia

The name of the **street** is next, followed by the **street number**. The next line in the address of an envelope contains the **codice postale** (*zip code* or *postal code*) known as the CAP in Italy. Then follows the name of the **city** or **town** the letter is going to, and, if appropriate, in parentheses the initials of the province. The name of the **country** is the last element and is placed by itself below the address. The **sender's address** is placed on the rear of the envelope preceded by the word: **Mittente** (*Sender*).

Body of a formal letter

If a letter is formal, and letterhead paper is not available, provide the sender's full information. In this case, the **sender's address** is written in the middle of the page and the **addressee's name and address** is placed below on the left-hand side.

> Telecom Italia
> Servizio Clienti Residenziali (*Residents' Service*)
> Casella Postale No. 117 (*P.O. Box No. 117*)
> 36100 Milano

Dott. Rossi Carlo
Via Bosco, 12
36100 Milano

The **place and date** are located in the middle of the page below the last line of the addressee's location.

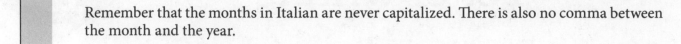

Milano, 12 novembre 2008

Remember that the months in Italian are never capitalized. There is also no comma between the month and the year.

Below the date is the reason for writing, or the **subject**.

SOGGETTO (*Subject*):

The opening **salutation** comes next. In Italian, titles are very important and should be used when known, and then followed by a comma. Here are some examples:

Egregio Signore,	*Dear Sir,*
Gentile Cliente,	*Dear Client,*
Gent.mo Dott. Giona,	*Very Kind Dr. Giona,*
Preg.issimo Sig. Rossi,	*Very Illustrious Mr. Rossi,*

The previous greetings are used to address a person one does not know well, or a person one needs to be respectful of. However, if the name or the title of the person being written to is unknown, instead of using these salutations address it to:

A chi di dovere,	*To whom it may concern,*
A chi di competenza,	*To whom it may concern,*

When dealing with government officials, the opening salutation would simply state their title, leaving out **Egregio** or **Gentile**. For example:

Sua Eccellenza (*His Excellency*)
Giorgio Napolitano
Presidente della Repubblica (*President of the Republic*)

Next in the letter there is an **introduction** giving the reason for writing, a **central paragraph** where the main topic is developed, **a conclusion**, **a closure**, and at the end the **signature** of the sender. Sometimes the address, the telephone number, and the e-mail are added. This last detail is put on the lower right side of the letter.

Body of an informal letter

An **informal letter** is almost the same format as a formal letter in Italian, except the **date and place of origin** are placed on the top of the page to the right. Unless someone has letterhead paper, no sender's address is placed on the page. A **salutation** is written on top of the page on the left and is always followed by a comma. The message is then started on a new line with a lowercase letter.

The formal closing expressions previously given do not work for informal letters. Instead, the ending of an informal letter is changed to an informal closing. Following are some closings that you will find useful in writing letters, both formal and informal:

Informal	
Affettuosamente	*With affection*
Affettuosi abbracci	*Affectionate hugs*
Affettuosi saluti	*With affection*
Baci e abbracci	*Hugs and kisses*
Baci affettuosi	*Affectionate kisses*
Con amicizia	*With friendship*

Formal	
Colgo l'occasione per porgere…	*Best regards*
Con stima	*With respect*
Cordiali saluti	*Cordially*
Distinti ossequi	*Distinguished greetings*
Distinti saluti	*Distinguished greetings*
In attesa di una Sua risposta	*Waiting for a reply*
Vi prego di gradire il nostro ringraziamento	*Please accept our thanks*
Vogliate accettare la nostra riconoscenza	*Please accept our gratitude*

If you forgot to write something in the letter, add it at the end by writing: **P.S.**, for **post scriptum** (*after writing*), and insert what was forgotten.

ESERCIZIO
19·1

Write the date, address, salutation, and closing for letters with the following information.

1. Roma / July 29 / Prof. Mario Ammirati (your cardiologist)

   _____

   _____

   _____

2. Venezia / January 16 / Anna Lolli (your cousin)

   _____

   _____

   _____

3. Milano / November 16 / Giacomo Rovelli (a client)

   _____

   _____

   _____

Abbreviations

Italian uses many abbreviations, especially in business letter writing. The more common abbreviations are the following:

All.	allegato	*attached*
ca.	circa	*about*
c.a.	corrente anno	*of this year*
CAP	codice postale	*zip code*
cc	copia conforme	*carbon copy*
c/c	conto corrente	*checking account*
c.m.	corrente mese	*of this month*
c/o	presso	*at*
C.P.	casella postale	*post office box*
CV	curriculum vitae	*résumé*
Ill.mo	illustrissimo	*most illustrious*
NB	nota bene	*note*
No.	numero	*number*
p.c.	per conoscenza	*knowing*
P.S.	post scriptum	*postscript*
p.v.	prossimo venturo	*next + time period (week, day, month)*
Sig.	Signor	*Mr.*
Sig.ra	Signora	*Mrs.*
S.p.A.	Società per azioni	*public limited company*
Spett.	Spettabile	*respectable*
Tel.	telefono	*telephone*
v.s.	vedi sopra	*see above*
Vs.	Vostro	*your*

E-mail

You may find that much of your correspondence is done through e-mail. Here is a list of useful vocabulary for sending messages online:

a	*to*	inserire	*to insert*
allegare	*to attach*	inviare	*to send*
cc	*copy*	inviare più tardi	*to send later*
comporre	*to compose*	messaggio elettronico	*e-mail message*
da	*from*	posta elettronica	*e-mail*
firma	*signature*	soggetto	*subject*

E-mail addresses and websites in Europe have endings that identify the country in which the address or the website is located. If it ends in **.it**, the country is Italy, if it ends in **.ch** it is Switzerland, and if it ends in **.at** Austria.

Forte@libero.at
zurich.ch
rai.it

Write a letter to your best friend in Perugia thanking her for her hospitality.

_____

_____

_____

_____

_____

_____

Write a letter to the Hotel Baglioni in Bologna to reserve a room, including addresses and the date.

_____

_____

_____

_____

_____

_____

_____

_____

_____

Let's write!

20

Now that you have expanded your ability to write, it is time to be creative and use what you have learned. Writing is a difficult skill for students learning a new language and for experts alike. It is possible for a language student to speak a language very well, but then find it difficult to write in the new language. Do not let this frustrate you. With practice, you will acquire better skills, and you will write more natural sounding Italian sentences. Let's start with some simple sentences and progress to more complex ones.

ESERCIZIO
20·1

Write a sentence for each grouping of words and phrases, using the tenses indicated in parentheses and providing your own words to enhance your sentences.

1. La gente / viaggiare / e visitare / i musei (present tense)

   _____

2. Immaginare / quando ero piccola / mi piacere / (imperfect)

   _____

3. A sciare / per il mio compleanno / imparare / (past perfect)

   _____

4. La casa / deve / imbiancare (passive voice)

   _____

5. Pensiamo che / avere / una vita più felice / lei volere (present subjunctive)

   _____

6. Cristina / molte volte /a casa / essere / dal lavoro / durante l'inverno (present perfect)

   _____

Complete the following sentences with the appropriate form of the verbs in parentheses.

1. Il Presidente dovrà lavorare molto per _____ la popolazione. (accontentare)

2. Questo fine settimana noi _____ a visitare i nostri amici. (andare)

3. La vita è piena di incertezze e di _____ . (cambiare)

4. C'è molto silenzio. Dove sono _____ a finire tutti? (andare)

5. Il libro che _____ è molto complesso, ma interessante. (leggere)

6. Sulle piste della neve la gente _____ fare attenzione. (dovere)

7. Perchè parli di tutti e non _____ niente di te stessa? (dire)

8. I due fratelli litigare sempre come _____ . (litigare)

Form original complete sentences, using the tenses suggested in parentheses.

1. _____ anche

   se _____ . (present)

2. _____

   benchè _____ . (future)

3. _____ tutt'al

   più _____ . (imperfect)

4. _____ più bella

   che _____ . (present perfect)

5. _____ più

   diretta _____ . (present)

6. _____ molto

   noiosa _____ . (past)

7. _____

   allorchè _____ . (future)

8. _____

   ma _____ . (present)

Write four phrases that could be answers to the interrogative words provided. You do not have to write complete sentences.

EXAMPLE: Chi?

Le mie amiche

Mio fratello e la sua fidanzata

I miei amici di scuola

Una signora con l'ombrello

1. Che cosa?

   a. _____

   b. _____

   c. _____

   d. _____

2. Perchè?

   a. _____

   b. _____

   c. _____

   d. _____

3. Come?

   a. _____

   b. _____

   c. _____

   d. _____

4. Dove?

   a. _____

   b. _____

   c. _____

   d. _____

5. Quando?

   a. _____

   b. _____

   c. _____

   d. _____

6. Quanto?

   a. _____

   b. _____

   c. _____

   d. _____

7. Quanto/Quanta/Quanti/Quante?

   a. _____

   b. _____

   c. _____

   d. _____

8. Quale/Quali?

   a. _____

   b. _____

   c. _____

   d. _____

Now it is time for you to launch into your own creative writing. Only some suggestions will be given on what to write, not how. The more you write and put into practice what you have learned, the more confident you will become. Your writing may be rusty at first, but keep at it, and in time you will create your own masterpiece.

ESERCIZIO
20·5

Write a paragraph describing in detail the home you live in. Include its size, the rooms, the furniture, how many people live in it, and its surroundings.

_____

_____

_____

_____

_____

_____

Write a paragraph that describes the best vacation you have ever taken. Give details of the location, how long you were there, what time of the year you visited, how many people went with you, and what made it so special.

_____

_____

_____

_____

_____

_____

_____

Write about yourself: where you were born, your education, your wishes, and hopes.

_____

_____

_____

_____

_____

_____

_____

Write a formal letter to the company you ordered your furniture from to inquire when it will be delivered.

_____

_____

_____

_____

_____

_____

_____

_____

Answer key

1 Declarative sentences and word order

1·1 1. P 2. S 3. S 4. P 5. P 6. S 7. S 8. S

1·2 1. Mio fratello è molto giovane. 2. Ha solo diciotto anni. 3. Si chiama Marco. 4. Ho parlato con lui ieri. 5. Lui è sempre puntuale. 6. Lui ti chiamerà presto. 7. Lei legge molti libri. 8. A noi (ci) piace Roma. 9. Vogliamo visitare porti nuovi. 10. Voi siete interessati ad imparare una lingua nuova.

1·3 1. Maria vive in questo palazzo. 2. Lucia, è la moglie di Pietro? 3. La casa di Marco è sulla spiaggia. 4. Lucia e suo marito rientrano dalle vacanze. 5. Abbiamo letto la notizia del tuo matrimonio sul giornale. 6. Ti piacciono il film di fantascienza. 7. Guardate la televisione alla sera? 8. Quando glielo portate? 9. Non andiamo, ma telefoniamo spesso. 10. La tazza del caffè è sul tavolino.

1·4 1. Oggi studiamo l'italiano. 2. Parliamo bene l'italiano. 3. Abbiamo già finito di leggere. 4. Studio raramente. 5. Glielo porterò questa sera. 6. Parliamo sempre dell'Italia. 7. Mi dà anche il caffè. 8. Porto un libro a mia sorella. 9. Ci incontriamo spesso per fare una festa. 10. Vivi in campagna ma ami la città.

1·5 1. A 2. N 3. A 4. A 5. N 6. N 7. N 8. A 9. A 10. N

1·6 1. The palms are tall and beautiful. 2. The moon is not shining today. 3. I see many stars in the sky. 4. At night the birds sleep in the trees. 5. I will never ever stay and sleep in this hotel. 6. Nobody says anything. 7. I do not like people who smoke. 8. He is afraid of traveling by plane. 9. We have a lot to do. 10. There is nothing I want to buy.

1·7 1. Mai 2. mai 3. nessuno 4. nè 5. nessuno 6. niente 7. nessuno 8. niente 9. Non 10. Mai, Non

1·8 1. Io non compro il vino in questo negozio. 2. L'impiegato mai è molto disponibile. 3. Maria non gioca con qualcuno. 4. Non mi piace guardare il baseball o il football alla televisione. 5. Nessuno di noi due sta bene. 6. Tu mai giochi a tennis. 7. I bambini di questo quartire mai sono fuori a giocare. 8. Gli studenti nelle scuole italiano non hanno sport o teatro. 9. Questa città non è vicina al mare o alle montagne. 10. Mai il mio lavoro è noioso.

2 Interrogative sentences

2·1 *Sample answers are provided.*   1. Cantano i ragazzi?   2. Lavora Luisa?   3. È grande la casa?   4. Viaggiano molto loro?   5. Dormite sempre voi?   6. Giocano a tennis le ragazze?   7. Piangono i bambini?   8. Fumi troppo tu?   9. È andata a casa Maria?   10. È ammalata la tua amica?

2·2 *Sample answers are provided.*   1. Giochi a pallacanestro?   2. Fumi tanto?   3. Abita qui Luigi?   4. Parli l'inglese?   5. Le signore giocano a bridge il mercoledì?   6. Viaggia in treno lei?   7. Sei felice in questa casa?   8. Tuo padre è l'uomo che ho incontrato l'altra sera?   9. Hai molto stress nella tua vita?   10. Hai viaggiato in molte parti del mondo?

2·3 *Sample answers are provided.*   1. Tu studi molto, giusto?   2. Suo marito è un campione di tennis, non è vero?   3. Loro sono in vacanza, no?   4. Il concerto è sabato, non è vero?   5. Preferisci il gelato al dolce, vero?   6. Loro vanno in chiesa la domenica, non è vero?   7. È molto scoraggiante perdere sempre, vero?   8. Se uno non paga le tasse, potrebbe andare in prigione, no?   9. I parchi americani sono molto belli, vero?   10. Bisogna viaggiare molte ore per attraversare gli Stati Uniti, giusto?

2·4 1. Per chi ha un libro Luisa?   2. Di chi è la casa?   3. A chi porti il pane?   4. Con chi vai al cinema?   5. Chi vogliono visitare?   6. Da chi stai quando vai in Florida?   7. A chi pensi spesso?   8. Chi viene domani?

2·5 1. a. Quando mangi il gelato? b. Quale gelato mangi? c. Perchè mangi il gelato? d. Mangi il gelato, non è vero?   2. a. Quando bevi il succo di frutta? b. Quale succo di frutta bevi? c. Perchè bevi il succo di frutta? d. Bevi il succo di frutta, giusto?   3. a. Quando mangi il formaggio? b. Quale formaggio mangi? c. Perchè mangi il formaggio? d. Mangi il formaggio, vero?   4. a. Quando mangi la pasta? b. Quale pasta mangi? c. Perchè mangi la pasta? d. Mangi la pasta, non è vero?   5. a. Quando bevi la cioccolata calda? b. Quale cioccolata calda bevi? c. Perchè bevi la cioccolata calda? d. Bevi la cioccolata calda, giusto?   6. a. Quando mangi la torta? b. Quale torta mangi? c. Perchè mangi la torta? d. Mangi la torta, vero?

2·6 1. Quante   2. Quando   3. Come   4. Quale   5. Chi   6. Quanti   7. Dove   8. Come   9. Da dove   10. Di dove

2·7 1. Chi   2. Di chi   3. A chi   4. Con chi   5. Da chi   6. Per chi   7. Di chi   8. Per chi   9. Di chi   10. A chi

2·8 *Sample answers are provided.*   1. Quando   2. Che cosa   3. Da dove   4. Quale   5. Che cosa   6. Quanti   7. Quante   8. Quali   9. Quando   10. Come

3 Questions and answers

3·1 1. a. Chi vuole andare in Italia? b. Dove vuole andare la vostra insegnante?   2. a. Quando sono chiuse le banche? b. Chi chiude il sabato e la domenica?   3. a. Che cosa costa troppo?   4. a. Che cosa annaffi tu?   5. a. Chi è seduto accanto alla sua padrona? b. Dove è seduto il cane?   6. a. Quando vai al cinema? b. Con chi vai al cinema domani?   7. a. Chi vuole visitare i figli?   8. a. Che cosa è parcheggiata davanti alla casa? b. Dov'è parcheggiata la macchina?   9. a. Chi vuole guardare il torneo di tennis? b. Che cosa vuole guardare tuo marito?   10. a. Chi ti telefona tutti i giorni? b. Che cosa fa tua sorella?

3·2   1. Vengo da Roma.   2. Oggi ne abbiamo dodici.   3. I ladri hanno rubato la televisione. 4. I miei amici viaggiano in macchina.   5. La mia sorella viene a visitarmi la prossima settimana.   6. Prima di andare in Italia, studio l'italiano.   7. Questi documenti sono dei miei genitori.   8. L'aereo arriva fra un'ora.   9. Ogni giorno leggo due giornali. 10. Faccio tutti questi costume per le cantanti d'opera.

3·3   1. Che cosa devono lavarsi i bambini?   2. Chi deve aspettare Maria?   3. Chi deve aspettare Maria?   4. Che cosa ha comprato lei?   5. Che cosa hai letto?   6. Che cosa ha perso tuo zio?   7. Che cosa ha dimenticato tua zia?   8. A che cosa pensi?   9. Chi ha freddo in classe?   10. Che cosa ha lasciato in classe Margherita?

3·4   1. La nonna abita con mio nonno.   2. Mia nonna guarda la televisione tutto il giorno. 3. Oggi ha telefonato il falegname.   4. Maria mi ha detto che non viene a casa mia. 5. Carlo va al mercato venerdì mattina.   6. Eric balla molto bene.   7. Il figlio della mia amica suona molto bene il piano.   8. Questa sera voglio mangiare gli spaghetti.

3·5   1. Lui viene al cinema con sua sorella?   2. Perchè non giochi con i bambini?   3. Quanti metri di stoffa ha comprato la sarta?   4. Quanto costa il nuovo CD?   5. Quale macchina hai comprato?   6. Che cosa avete mangiato questa sera?   7. Siete andati a mangiare al ristorante?   8. Da dove è venuto questo libro?

3·6   *Sample answers are provided.*   1. a. Quando vai al parco? b. Ci vado quando ritorno a casa dal lavoro.   2. a. Perchè devi partire così presto? b. Perchè non mi piace viaggiare con il buio.   3. a. Da dove viene quel dottore famoso? b. Viene da Firenze.   4. a. Chi hai portato a casa ieri? b. Ho portato il mio ragazzo.   5. a. Come vai all'aereoporto? b. Devo prendere un tassì.   6. a. Da quanto tempo studiate in Italia? b. Da diversi anni.   7. a. Quale delle due ragazze conosci meglio? b. Quella vicina alla porta.   8. a. Quanto tempo ci vuole per arrivare in Australia? b. Ci vogliono più di venti ore di areo.

4   Imperatives

4·1   1. Bevi!, beva!, bevano!   2. aspetta!, aspetti!, aspettino!   3. ordina!, ordini!, ordinino! 4. sta'!, stia!, stiano!   5. vota!, voti!, votino!   6. leggi!, legga!, leggano!   7. mangia!, mangi!, mangino!   8. sappi!, sappia!, sappiano!   9. sii!, sia!, siano!   10. metti!, metta!, mettano!

4·2   1. Spingere!   2. Tirare!   3. Non toccare!   4. Non calpestare l'erba!   5. Non parlare all'autista!   6. Non fare fotografie!   7. Non oltrepassare!   8. Non parcheggiare! 9. Non dar da mangiare agli animali!   10. Tenere la porta chiusa!

4·3   1. Let's go to the movies!   2. Let him travel to Europe!   3. Let her speak!   4. Let's write a letter to Grandmother!   5. Let him do what he wants!   6. Let me speak!   7. Let's go get a coffee!   8. Let me eat!   9. Let's read!   10. Let's take a picture! 11. Let the others speak! 12. Let me stay!

4·4   1. Non mangiate tutti i cioccolatini!   2. Non compriamo le ciliege!   3. Non fate la doccia!   4. Non salutare il professore!   5. Non facciamo gli esercizi!   6. Non chiamare un tassì!   7. Non parlare lentamente!   8. Non mettete la giacca!   9. Non comprate una giacca pesante!   10. Non imparare a usare il computer!

4·5   1. parli   2. Scrivi   3. chiudete   4. provi   5. Studiate   6. Prepara   7. Cuocia 8. Compra   9. Aspettino   10. Controlla

4·6   1. riposarti   2. alzarti   3. Fermatevi   4. si rivolga   5. pettinati   6. svegliatevi
7. Copritevi   8. Si accomodino   9. dimenticatevi   10. si porti

4·7   1. Dille che lui l'ama!   2. Stammi vicino!   3. Dicci chi viene alla festa!   4. Dammi
la borsa!   5. Dacci un colpo di telefono!   6. Facci un favore!   7. Fagli un regalo per il
suo compleanno!   8. Non dargli un orologio!   9. Dalle la macchina nuova!   10. Non
darle la macchina fotografica!

5   Coordinating conjunctions

5·1   *Sample answers are provided.*   1. e   2. ma   3. ma   4. o   5. e   6. ma   7. perciò
8. quindi   9. e   10. per questo

5·2   *Sample answers are provided.*   1. Ci sono tanti nostri amici e vorremmo che venissi anche
tu.   2. Ti ammonisco, ma fa quel che vuoi.   3. Segui il tuo istinto, ma non venire a
piangere da me.   4. Filippo non è generoso, infatti è molto tirchio.   5. Franco è un
ragazzo molto intelligente, infatti è un genio.   6. Tu vuoi andare al cinema, ma io non
voglio andarci.   7. I miei genitori non vogliono comprarmi un cane e neppure un gatto.
8. Se tutto va bene mi comprerò la moto, e mi comprerò la macchina l'anno prossimo.
9. Abbiamo comprato la frutta e la carne, però abbiamo dimenticato il pane.   10. Lui non
sta molto bene, per questo deve andare dal dottore per un controllo.

5·3   1. però   2. e   3. quindi   4. perciò   5. però   6. e   7. però   8. ma   9. e   10. e

5·4   *Sample answers are provided.*   1. Entrambi Luigi ed io andremo alla festa.   2. I soldi e il
potere non portano la felicità.   3. Ci ha dato dei regali, e ci ha invitati a casa sua.   4. Era
stanco, e non si sentiva bene.   5. Ho finito i miei compiti, quindi posso andare fuori a
giocare.   6. Vi vedrò tutti fra due settimane o per Natale.   7. Il ladro si mosse
velocemente e silenziosamente.   8. Nè io nè te, possiamo andare al matrimonio.   9. Oggi
ha fatto freddo, infatti ha nevicato.   10. Uscirai con i tuoi amici o con i tuoi parenti?

6   Subordinating conjunctions

6·1   *Sample answers are provided.*   1. perchè   2. benchè   3. prima che   4. dopo che   5. a
patto che   6. Se   7. che   8. perchè

6·2   1. come   2. Benchè   3. perchè   4. perchè   5. così... che   6. perchè   7. sebbene
8. Benchè

6·3   1. Se   2. Benchè   3. ma   4. quindi   5. perchè   6. Dopo che   7. perchè
8. Dato che

6·4   1. e   2. Benchè   3. benchè, perchè, così   4. sebbene   5. e, ma, perchè   6. e, anche
7. o   8. Benchè, e

7   Relative pronouns

7·1   1. che   2. che   3. che   4. che   5. che   6. chi   7. chi   8. chi

7·2   1. di cui   2. da cui   3. il cui   4. in cui   5. per cui   6. in cui   7. a cui   8. di cui

7·3   1. che   2. chi   3. quello che   4. di cui   5. Chi   6. in cui   7. da cui   8. che

7·4 1. quanto 2. dove 3. Chi 4. chiunque 5. Chi 6. Quelli che 7. Chiunque 8. quello che

7·5 1. che 2. che 3. chi 4. chi 5. di cui 6. a cui 7. con cui 8. quello che

7·6 1. Chi 2. che 3. cui 4. che 5. cui 6. Chiunque 7. chi 8. dove (in cui)

8 Present and past participles

8·1 1. assistente (*assistant*) 2. commovente (*emotionally moving*) 3. dirigente (*directing, director*) 4. mancante (*missing*) 5. obbediente (*obedient*) 6. perdente (*losing*) 7. riposante (*restful, resting*) 8. tollerante (*tolerant*) 9. uscente (*exiting*) 10. vivente (*living*)

8·2 1. bollente 2. corrente 3. sorridente 4. obbedienti 5. assistente 6. sconvolgente 7. divertente 8. seguente

8·3 1. governanti 2. dipendente 3. emigranti 4. conducenti 5. passanti 6. dissetante 7. partecipanti 8. abbaglianti

8·4 1. fritte 2. mosso 3. preceduto 4. accaldato 5. depurate 6. ridotta 7. amata 8. conosciuto

8·5 1. fermata 2. permesso 3. visto 4. invitati 5. soffritto 6. candidati 7. ammalati 8. udito

8·6 1. Quando sarà finito il concerto, ti riporteremo a casa. 2. Appena saranno spente le luci, la bambina si addormenterà. 3. Quando avranno finito il corso, gli studenti andranno al mare. 4. Quando saranno saliti sull'autobus, troveranno senz'altro un posto a sedere. 5. Appena avranno lavato i piatti, puliranno la cucina. 6. Quando avranno preso la patente, potranno guidare. 7. Quando saranno arrivati a destinazione, si riposeranno. 8. Appena finiti i compiti, potranno andare fuori a giocare.

8·7 1. Finitala, mi sono sentita sollevata. 2. Riposatosi, viene a visitarvi. 3. Cercava la palla dappertutto, trovatala è uscito a giocare. 4. Le ho lette tutte in questi giorni. 5. Li vedo sempre quando ritornano dal lavoro. 6. La cioccolata calda era squisita, ne ho bevute due tazze. 7. Ne ho mangiata una, ma era acerba. 8. Ne ho comprate tante.

9 Adjectives

9·1 *Sample answers are provided.* 1. lungo, interessante, triste 2. giallo, piccolo, estivo 3. grande, bianca, stretta 4. nero, robusto, piccolo 5. alta, pericolosa, vasta 6. quotidiano, interessante, diurno 7. bianca, fredda, nuova 8. intelligente, felice, longilineo

9·2 1. Ho visto una povera donna bloccata nella neve. 2. Sono bambini americani. 3. Lui è un cittadino austriaco. 4. Mi piacciono i tavoli quadrati. 5. Nel Michigan si trova terreno sabbioso dappertutto. 6. Lei indossa solo scarpe nere. 7. Ho una sciarpa rossa. 8. Lei è una persona malata.

9·3 1. incertezza 2. bellezza 3. fioritura 4. difficoltà 5. velocità 6. novità 7. calore 8. realtà 9. veleno 10. profumo 11. freschezza

9·4   1. i rosso·neri   2. il futuro   3. i mondiali   4. stranieri   5. I ricchi, i belli   6. gli studiosi   7. i temerari, deboli   8. I timidi

9·5   1. Gli sportivi   2. chiaro, tondo   3. toscano, fiorentina   4. piano, sano, lontano   5. il peggio   6. gli stranieri   7. le cinesi, duro   8. il futuro

9·6   1. più alto di   2. molto alto   3. meno di   4. pochissimo   5. più, della   6. molto salata   7. più, della   8. molto fredda

9·7   1. a. Il gatto è più piccolo del cane nero. b. Il gatto è il più piccolo di tutti. c. Il gatto è piccolissimo.   2. a. Il dolce è più buono del gelato. b. Il dolce è il migliore di tutti. c. Il dolce è buonissimo.   3. a. L'uomo è più alto di sua moglie. b. L'uomo è il più alto di tutti. c. L'uomo è altissimo.   4. a. L'inverno è più freddo dell'autunno. b. L'inverno è la stagione più fredda di tutte. c. L'inverno è freddissimo.

9·8   1. giovanissima   2. molto vecchia   3. molto interessante   4. molto indaffarata   5. più ambizioso che   6. molto vecchia   7. vecchissimi   8. molto ricchi

9·9   1. piovana   2. nudo   3. sereno   4. insipida   5. disoccupato   6. primaverile   7. arida   8. orfano

10   Adverbs

10·1   1. esattamente   2. doppiamente   3. ordinatamente   4. freddamente   5. velocemente   6. attivamente   7. allegramente   8. pacificamente

10·2   1. felici   2. felicemente   3. esatta   4. ordinatamente   5. freddo   6. freddamente   7. attiva   8. attivamente

10·3   *Sample answers are provided.*   1. a dirotto   2. fuori   3. davanti   4. fortunatamente   5. poi   6. molto   7. dintorni   8. circa

10·4   *Sample answers are provided.*   1. profondamente   2. attentamente   3. diligentemente   4. velocemente   5. molto   6. attentamente   7. continuamente   8. frequentemente

10·5   1. più diligentemente   2. moltissimo   3. benissimo   4. più tardi   5. più volentieri   6. peggio   7. malissimo   8. molto elegantemente

11   Pronouns

11·1   1. a. La portano al cinema. b. Portano lei al cinema.   2. a. Luisa li porta in piscina tutti i giorni. b. Luisa porta loro in piscina tutti i giorni.   3. a. Lo contatterò appena posso. b. Contatterò lui appena posso.   4. a. Lo portiamo all'aereoporto, poi torniamo a casa. b. Portiamo lui all'aereoporto poi torniamo a casa.   5. a. Ci inviti a cena a casa tua. b. Inviti noi a cena a casa tua.   6. a. Luigi li porta in vacanza. b. Luigi porta loro in vacanza.   7. a. Li vediamo al mare. b. Vediamo loro al mare.   8. a. Lo rivedo con molto piacere. b. Rivedo lui con molto piacere.

11·2   1. uno (In treno ho parlato con uno che non conoscevo.)   2. Uno (Uno non sa mai cosa dire ai parenti dei morti.)   3. una (Abbiamo conosciuto una che parla bene l'inglese.)   4. Uno (Uno ha avuto problemi di cuore mentre era in aereo.)   5. uno (Ho parlato con uno dell'anagrafe.)   6. uno (Non c'è uno che capisca la matematica.)   7. una (Ho parlato con una che non mi piaceva affatto.)   8. una (Maria è una che sa il fatto suo.)   9. una (Teresa è una delle mie migliori amiche.)

11·3   1. chiunque   2. Ognuno   3. Chiunque   4. Qualcuno   5. Chiunque   6. ognuno   7. qualcuno   8. qualcuno

11·4   *Sample answers are provided.*   1. niente   2. niente   3. qualcosa   4. Nessuno   5. qualcosa   6. nessuno   7. qualcosa   8. nulla

11·5   1. mi, ti   2. si   3. si   4. ci   5. vi   6. mi   7. Mi   8. si

12   Infinitives

12·1   1. a. Prima di comprare, chiediamo il prezzo. b. Dopo aver chiesto il prezzo, compriamo. 2. a. Prima di telefonare a Marco, chiamo un taxi. b. Dopo aver telefonato a Marco, chiamo un taxi.   3. a. Prima di passare di qui, vado in chiesa. b. Dopo essere passato di qui, vado in chiesa.   4. a. Prima di mangiare, mi lavo le mani. b. Dopo essermi lavato le mani, mangio.   5. a. Prima di agire, pensa. b. Dopo aver pensato, agisce.   6. a. Prima di andare a lavorare, mi vesto. b. Dopo essermi vestito, vado a lavorare.   7. a. Prima di andare alla posta, scrive la lettera. b. Dopo aver scritto la lettera, va alla posta.   8. a. Prima di giocare, studiamo. b. Dopo aver studiato, giochiamo.

12·2   1. vedere   2. essere   3. giocare   4. fumare   5. bere   6. andare   7. fare   8. vedervi

12·3   1. vedere   2. averci pensato   3. arrivare   4. chiamare   5. aver finito   6. comprare   7. passare   8. passare

12·4   1. aver appreso   2. diventare   3. aver letto   4. andare   5. aver finito   6. aver telefonato   7. guardare   8. diventare

12·5   1. Sua madre non può bere vino.   2. La ragazza non può mai leggere.   3. Dopo pranzo possiamo andare a riposare.   4. Lei non può aprire la porta a nessuno.   5. Noi possiamo parlare con i nostri amici.   6. Lei ha potuto comprare i biglietti per l'aereo.   7. Voi siete potuti andare dal dottore.   8. Io posso farmi la barba tutte le mattine.

12·6   1. parlare   2. camminare   3. suonare   4. comprare   5. pulire   6. arrivare   7. vedere   8. ascoltare

13   Words with special meaning

13·1   1. Allora   2. quindi   3. Dunque   4. Come   5. infatti   6. Allora   7. quindi   8. infatti

13·2   1. mica   2. mica   3. affatto   4. affatto   5. mica   6. mica   7. affatto   8. mica

13·3   1. Su   2. giù   3. su   4. Avanti   5. Su   6. indietro   7. indietro   8. Avanti

13·4   *Sample answers are provided.*   1. Certamente!   2. Mamma mia!   3. Santo cielo!   4. Chiedo scusa!   5. Acqua in bocca!   6. È incredibile!   7. Davvero?   8. Non c'è di chè.

13·5 *Sample answers are provided.* 1. Ho visto tanti cigni nel lago. 2. Sai dove sono le scarpe di tua figlia? 3. Non riesci a farcela ad arrivare in cima alla collina? 4. Il corridore è caduto poco prima di arrivare al traguardo. 5. Non so dove è andata a finire la mia amica. 6. Avete finito la relazione per il direttore? 7. Sperate di andare a sciare questo inverno? 8. Quanto rumore c'è in questo bar!

14 Idioms and special phrases

14·1 1. volentieri 2. ben volentieri 3. sento 4. posso 5. posso 6. d'accordo 7. d'accordo 8. volentieri, posso

14·2 *Sample answers are provided.* 1. Non voglio più vederti a casa mia. 2. Non mi chiama mai. 3. Finalmente sei arrivato. 4. Non fai altro che parlare. 5. Non dire a nessuno quello che ti ho detto. 6. Non ha ancora molta esperienza. 7. Si compra tutto in quel negozio. 8. Mio figlio non sa risparmiare.

14·3 1. comportano male 2. Vattene 3. arrangiati 4. Mi spremo il cervello 5. si è fatta male 6. Muoviti 7. impicciarsi degli affari 8. sistemo nell'appartamento

15 Antonyms and contrasts

15·1 *Sample answers are provided.* 1. No, l'ho spenta. 2. No, venerdì lavoro. 3. No, l'ha aggiustata. 4. No, l'abbiamo venduta. 5. No, ho pianto. 6. No, l'ha chiusa. 7. No, l'ho spinta. 8. No, sono scesi.

15·2 1. le tragedie 2. l'entrata 3. libertà 4. morte 5. salute 6. odio 7. salita, discesa, 8. giorno, notte 9. domande, risposte 10. guerra, pace

15·3 *Sample answers are provided.* 1. Il viaggio non è lungo, è corto. 2. Questo ristorante non è pulito, è sporco. 3. Lei non è sempre felice. Qualche volta è infelice. 4. Lui è magro, ma lei è grassa. 5. Il libro non è interessante. È molto noioso. 6. Il pacco che spedisco non è leggero. È molto pesante. 7. Questo esercizio non è facile, è difficile. 8. Suo padre era ricco, ma adesso è povero.

16 Passive voice

16·1 1. Il programma televisivo è guardato dai bambini. 2. Il bar è gestito da Giovanni. 3. La casa nuova è comprata da mia figlia. 4. Il libro è scritto dal professore di italiano. 5. Il nuovo romanzo giallo è letto dagli studenti. 6. Questo bel palazzo è costruito da un famoso architetto. 7. Il viaggio in Asia è fatto dai miei amici. 8. La birra è bevuta da Luigi.

16·2 1. Da chi viene prenotato l'albergo? 2. Da chi vengono indirizzate le lettere? 3. Da chi viene interpretato il film? 4. Da chi viene organizzata la festa? 5. Da chi vengono inviati questi pacchi? 6. Da chi viene firmato il documento? 7. Da chi viene pagato il conto? 8. Da chi viene preparata la cena?

16·3 1. L'albergo viene prenotato da mio fratello. 2. Le lettere vengono indirizzate dalla segretaria. 3. Il film viene interpretato da Sofia Loren. 4. La festa viene organizzata dai miei amici. 5. Questi pacchi vengono inviati dalla mamma. 6. Il documento viene firmato dal notaio.   7. Il conto viene pagato da mio padre.   8. La cena viene preparata dalla cuoca.

16·4   1. va spenta   2. va spalata   3. va buttato   4. vanno asciugati   5. va controllato   6. vanno lodati   7. vanno aiutati   8. vanno lavati

16·5   1. Si lavora per vivere.   2. Si è lavorato per tanti anni per avere un certo benessere.   3. Si sono piantati tanti fiori per avere un bel giardino.   4. Di notte, si vedono tante stelle.   5. Si porteranno tante cose in Italia per le nostre nipoti.   6. In America si vive bene.   7. In questa casa si parla solo l'italiano.   8. Negli aeroporti si vedono tante cose strane.

17   Subjunctive mood

17·1   1. faccia   2. stia   3. esca, vada   4. sia   5. arrivi   6. faccia   7. ritorniate   8. dormiamo

17·2   1. abbia fatto   2. abbiano vinto   3. abbia conosciuto   4. abbiate mangiato   5. abbia trascurato   6. abbiate letto   7. abbia nevicato   8. abbiate ricevuto

17·3   1. facessi   2. vincessero   3. avessi   4. mangiaste   5. trascurasse   6. piacesse   7. nevicasse   8. ricevessi

17·4   1. avesse studiato   2. aveste fatto   3. foste venuti   4. fossero, andati   5. io fossi arrivato   6. avessi venduto   7. fossi partito   8. fosse piaciuto

17·5   1. sapessi   2. vedessi   3. abbiate   4. Si accomodi   5. stiano   6. Pensi   7. aiuti   8. dormissi

17·6   *Sample answers are provided.*   1. Benchè   2. dovunque   3. Sebbene   4. purchè   5. Benchè   6. Benchè   7. Prima che   8. affinchè

17·7   1. impariate   2. imparassi   3. stiate   4. fosse stata   5. ascoltiamo   6. dia   7. chiami   8. metta

17·8   *Sample answers are provided.*   1. tu ti prepari in fretta   2. il bambino si addormenti presto   3. tu parli bene l'inglese   4. venga un temporale   5. tu non finisca gli esercizi   6. si laureino presto   7. mi mandino un messaggio   8. possiate visitarci

17·9   1. avessi potuto   2. avessi chiamato   3. avessi   4. avessi avuto   5. studiaste   6. avessero studiato   7. parli   8. piaccia

18   Punctuation

18·1   1. Il Sig. Fortina, non si è presentato per l'appuntamento.   2. Il film, che abbiamo visto insieme, ha vinto l'Oscar.   3. Maria ha trent'anni. Vive sola in una grande città.   4. No, non vengo a casa tua domani.   5. Dunque, per finire, dico che bisogna parlare chiaramente.   6. Vorrei vedere le chiese, i musei e i parchi di Roma.   7. Mi piace viaggiare, ma ho paura di viaggiare in aereo.   8. È venuto anche Luigi, lo zio di Marco.

18·2   1. Chi sono quelle persone?   2. No, certo.   3. Dunque, quel ragazzo è un pittore.   4. Dove vai? Vado all'aereoporto.   5. Quanta gente c'è per la strada! Dove vanno?   6. Il mio lavoro è noioso, poco interessante, statico e facile.   7. Mia sorella disse: "Mi piacerebbe andare a sciare, ma non c'è abbastanza neve".   8. Io studio tanto, ma non ricordo niente.

18·3 *Sample answers are provided.*   1. Oggi ho mangiato: la minestra, la carne, la verdure e il dolce.   2. Vuoi andare a fare una passeggiata con noi?   3. Guarda come è grigio il cielo!   4. Anna mi chiese: "Vuoi andare al mercato venerdì?"   5. Hai sentito la novità...?   6. La figlia del Senatore *** non si è presentata all'appuntamento.   7. Marco si è alzato tardi (del resto fa sempre così), ed è arrivato al lavoro in ritardo.   8. La partita Juventus-Roma è stata sospesa per il maltempo.

18·4 1. L'amica di mia mamma è molto simpatica.   2. Quell'oggetto in vetrina è molto bello.   3. Vorrei parlargli a quattr'occhi.   4. Non l'ho ascoltata perchè chiacchieravo.   5. Non hai dato un bell'esempio ai tuoi figli.   6. Luisa ha cercato di seguire le istruzioni alla bell'e meglio.   7. L'alunna non ha finito l'esame.   8. Lei compra l'oca al supermercato.

18·5 1. un po' di pane   2. ciascun'alunna   3. buon anno   4. non date nessun consiglio   5. dottor Gavozzi   6. gran serata   7. sant'Anna   8. ancor niente   9. ben fatto   10. buon giorno

18·6 1. da'   2. sta'   3. Va'   4. To'   5. be'   6. ve'   7. Di'   8. po'

19 Letter writing

19·1 *Sample answers are provided.*
1. Roma, 29 luglio
    Gent.mo Prof. Mario Ammirati,
    Distinti ossequi,
2. Venezia, 16 gennaio
    Carissima Anna,
    Baci affettuosi,
3. Milano, 16 novembre
    Gentile cliente,
    Con stima,

19·2 *Sample letter is provided.*

Cara Teresa,

*   ti scrivo per ringraziarti per la tua ospitalità durante il nostro soggiorno in Italia. Siamo stati molto bene con te. La tua casa è molto bella e comoda. Il panorama è meraviglioso. Ti ringraziamo per essere stata così gentile da averci portati in giro per Perugia e averci fatto vedere i posti più caratteristici della città.*

*   Abbiamo passato una vacanza indimenticabile grazie a te e a tuo marito. Speriamo di rivederci presto. Intanto ti mandiamo i nostri più cari saluti e di nuovo molte grazie.*

Con affetto,

Luisa e Giovanni

19·3 *Sample letter is provided.*

Giovanni Beltrame
3315 Bright Street
Boston, MA 20315

Hotel Baglioni
Via Indipendenza 33
Bologna 44134

15.03.2009

A chi di competenza,

Invio questa mia, per richiedere informazioni sulla disponibilità di una camera doppia per due persone, per tre notti, dal 15 al 18 luglio.

Vi sarei grato se poteste mandarmi le informazioni richieste includendo il listino prezzi il più presto possibile.

In attesa di una vostra risposta,

invio cordiali saluti,

Giovanni Beltrame

20 Let's write!

20·1 *Sample answers are provided.* 1. La gente viaggia e visita i musei di tutto il mondo. A quasi tutti piace vedere l'arte. 2. Quando ero piccola mi piaceva immaginare di essere una principessa, con vestiti e parrucche molto belli. 3. Per il mio compleanno avevo imparato a sciare, poi sono caduta e da allora ho sempre avuto paura di sciare. 4. La casa deve essere imbiancata, ma prima devo staccare tutti i quadri dai muri. 5. Pensiamo che lei voglia avere una vita più felice, ma non riesce a trovare quello vuole. 6. Cristina è stata a casa dal lavoro molte volte durante l'inverno. Il dottore le ha dato gli antibiotici, ma lei non li ha presi.

20·2 1. accontentare 2. andremo 3. cambiamenti 4. andati 5. leggete 6. deve fare attenzione 7. e non dici 8. litigano

20·3 *Sample answers are provided.* 1. Vengo anche se non ho molto tempo. 2. Verrò benchè non ne abbia molta voglia. 3. Ti compro un divano, tutt'al più se non ti piace lo riporto indietro. 4. Ho visto una nave più bella che grande. 5. Ti mando per la strada più diretta e più corta che posso. 6. La conferenza di quel famoso dottore, è stata molto noiosa, ma molto educativa. 7. Saprò chi verrà allorchè avrò ricevuto tutte le prenotazioni. 8. Io studio molto, ma non ricordo quasi niente.

20·4 *Sample answers are provided.* 1. a. Una borsa nuova b. Un vestito e le scarpe c. La macchina rossa d. La televisione moderna 2. a. Sono stanca b. Hanno studiato molto c. Non sto bene d. Ho sonno 3. a. Sto bene b. In macchina c. Mi chiamo Maria d. Vanno bene 4. a. Al mercato b. In vacanza c. Vicino al ristorante d. In centro 5. a. Domani

mattina b. Più tardi c. Fra due settimane d. Appena posso   6. a. Costa troppo b. Due mesi
c. Non costa molto d. Sempre   7. a. Ho tre figli. b. Voglio poca pasta. c. Solo tre amici
d. Tre paste   8. a. Il libro a destra b. Non mi piace nessun ristorante. c. Preferisco il cibo
italiano. d. I miei vecchi amici

20·5   *Sample answer is provided.*

La mia casa si trova in un piccolo paese vicino a una grande città. È una casa moderna e grande, ma non troppo. Ci sono: quattro camere da letto, tre bagni, un bel soggiorno, la sala da pranzo e una cucina spaziosa con tutti i piani di cottura in granito. È una casa molto luminosa perchè ha le finestre molto grandi. I mobili sono nuovi e moderni. In questa casa ci abitano solo due persone. La casa è circondata da alberi e da un bel giardino con tante piante e fiori di tutte le specie

20·6   *Sample answer is provided.*

La mia vacanza favorita è stata quella di tanti anni fa sulle Dolomiti in Italia. Sono andata con la mia famiglia in quel posto meraviglioso a sciare. Abbiamo sciato per una settimana intera dalla mattina fino a tardo pomeriggio. La neve era bellissima, il cielo era sempre azzurro, e le montagne maestose erano coperte di neve. Le piste dove abbiamo sciato erano preparate tutte le mattine. Alcune erano difficili, altre erano facili, e mi potevo rilassare e godere il panorama. Le Dolomiti offrono un vastissimo territorio dove sciare. Non dimenticherò mai quella settimana con la mia famiglia.

20·7   *Sample answer is provided.*

Io sono nata in Africa e precisamente ad Addis Abeba, che è la capitale dell'Etiopia. Ho studiato sia in Etiopia che in Italia. Ho preso la laurea di insegnamento e poi ho continuato e ho preso una seconda laurea in lingue. Mi piaceva molto studiare. Quando mi sono laureata ho dovuto decidere se insegnare o fare l'interprete e la traduttrice. Ho deciso di insegnare. Mi sarebbe piaciuto anche fare l'interprete.

Oggi desidero e spero di comprare una casetta in Italia dove potrei andare in vacanza con la mia famiglia. La mia speranza è quella di avere tutta la mia famiglia unita in un posto per un certo periodo di tempo. Questo forse rimarrà solo un desiderio perchè hanno tutti la loro vita e le loro attività, ma io continuo a sperare.

20·8 *Sample letter is provided.*

Luisa Marconi
Via Tornabuoni 53
40132 Firenze
Italia

Firenze 23 aprile 2009

Spett. le Ditta
Natuzzi
Via Maggiore 35
40134 Bologna
Italia
SOGGETTO: Informazioni su ordine inviato
A chi di dovere,

    Scrivo per avere informazioni sull'ordine mandatoVi tre settimane fa. Vorrei sapere se l'ordine Vi è arrivato, e quando posso aspettare di ricevere la merce ordinata. Vorrei farVi presente che ho urgenza di ricevere i mobili richiesti, perchè mi sposo fra due settimane e vorrei avere la casa ben sistemata.

Vi sarei infinitamente grato se poteste mandarmi una risposta.

    In attesa, invio distinti ossequi,

    Luigi Franchetti